Dr Ajit Gomez is a retired Consultant Psychiatrist in the UK. Whilst in this job, he pursued an inner call to enter the Diaconate Formation Programme under the Archdiocese of Birmingham, UK, and was ordained a deacon in 2013. He responded to a second call to work as a Roman Catholic Prison Chaplain in 2019, after taking early retirement from the NHS. He is very passionate about the message of peace and forgiveness offered by Jesus Christ and aspires to live up to the calling to serve the Lord, by word and deed.

I would like to dedicate this work to the entire prison population in the world; especially those who have responded to the love of God that reached them within the confines of the prison.

It was the spiritual hunger among the prison population and my outreach to them that ignited this work.

Ajit Gomez

# THE OUTSTRETCHED ARM OF LOVE

AUSTIN MACAULEY PUBLISHERS®

LONDON • CAMBRIDGE • NEW YORK • SHARJAH

A CIP catalogue record for this title is available from the British Library.

ISBN 9781035825752 (Paperback)
ISBN 9781035825769 (ePub e-book)

www.austinmacauley.com

First Published 2024
Austin Macauley Publishers Ltd®
1 Canada Square
Canary Wharf
London
E14 5AA

This work could not have been started without the support of my wife, Sheeja, who has been a pillar of support to me all through my parish and prison ministry. My gratitude is due to my sister, Manju, who was keenly involved in correcting errors in the manuscript and gave me the confidence to go ahead with the publication. I have always had efficacious prayer support from my sisters, Jayanthi and Geetha. My children and their spouses, Priyanka and Sam; together with David and Annie, encouraged me in this effort with their best wishes and prayers. The love for my grandchildren, Jonah, Ethan, Zara and Jadon, provided the impetus for this work. In addition, the Prison Chaplaincy Team, the Harborne Prayer Group and Lay Ministers, Claire and David Hallam from the Methodist Church have stood by me through difficult times, to ensure that I have a good outcome in all my endeavours. My gratitude to Fr Peter Conley for the direction he provided in shaping the literary, grammatical and theological composition of this book.

Above all, it was the grace of our Lord Jesus Christ and the love of God working through the Holy Spirit, that was instrumental in beginning the work and bringing it to completion.

# Preface

As we journey through the aftermath of 'the pandemic', the consequences of the long drawn out Russian-Ukraine War, alongside the recession in the UK, with soaring energy bills and petrol prices, the voice of Almighty God has been a constant reliable fortress for man to take refuge in these days of darkness and turmoil.

I was specially blessed during the long period of lockdown in the UK from March 2020 up to the dawn of 2022, because my ministry in the prison took on a new dimension. The cancelled services and other regular group activities meant more time for one-to-one ministry. Almost every Sunday for nearly a year, I was able to provide spiritual nourishment, for about 50 prisoners. This was in the form of weekly reflection on the Sunday Gospel, which were posted through the cell doors, along with the Mass Readings and the prayers. This set of 33 reflections is entirely Christ-centred, based on Scripture references from the Holy Bible and the teaching found in the Catechism of the Catholic Church (CCC quotes in textbox for each chapter). I have included excerpts of real-life stories, material from Christian talks in the Internet (in italics), together with my own knowledge of being brought up as a 'cradle Catholic' and then maturing into 'a Renewed Catholic'.

My faith took a steep upward climb in 1993, followed by 'ups and downs' in my faith, during the turn of the century to the third millennium. A deeper exploration of the Christian truth led me to delve more deeply into Pentecostal and Protestant thinking and spirituality. However, my perseverance in seeking the guidance of the Holy Spirit brought me back more strongly to the Holy Catholic Church culminating in my ordination as a Permanent Deacon in the Catholic Church in 2013.

I hope that these short reflections will both inspire and increase the faith, of not merely the prison population to whom it was addressed but also help both clergy and laity in sharing our faith. I hope this will contribute to greater unity in the Church and undo any divisive spirit of the Reformation, whilst upholding the depth of faith and love of Scripture, so close to the heart of millions of non-Catholic Christians.

My prayer is to echo the words of Jesus in John 17:22 'we may all be one just as the Father and I are one', which underlines the universality (catholicity) of our faith in the Son of God who took human form to visit us; so that Heaven and Earth may be woven through the passage of time, into one unblemished fabric of love, as the prophetic exhortations of the Holy Bible are being fulfilled even today, in Christ Jesus Our Lord and Saviour.

My prayer is for the Lord to grant the grace for many to be enriched and blessed, with perceptible signs and wonders, as the contents of these reflections provide encouragement for us to grow closer to Our God, to whom we must all give an account of our lives.

Ajit Gomez

# Accept Your Cross

The Bible verse to remember and understand is Matthew 16:24: "If anyone wants to be a follower of mine, let him renounce himself and take up his cross and follow me."

The cross is the symbol or logo of Christianity and stands for the capital punishment or death penalty by crucifixion in the Roman Empire. Jesus Christ is known for his sinless life marked by good deeds, miracles and suffering to the point of death on a cross.

Jesus took all our sins on the cross along with our guilt and shame and died in our place. Jesus paid the ransom price for our sins on the cross with his precious blood (1 Peter 1:18-19). The Bible says that we have been bought by the blood of Christ and washed in his blood of all our sins. Jesus, the Son of God, suffered for us and such is the great love of God for all mankind.

This is the true story of Fr Maximillian Kolbe and Franciszek Gajowniczek to explain the meaning of Jesus dying in our place:

*Mr Gajowniczek was one of several prisoners selected by the Nazis to die by starvation in a dungeon at Auschwitz called the 'hunger bunker'. He survived because Fr Maximillian Kolbe volunteered to take his place!*

*The punishment was imposed by the Germans because another inmate had escaped. Mr Gajowniczek, a farmer in civilian life, pleaded that he should be spared because he had a wife and children.*

*Mr Gajowniczek told the story himself: Father Kolbe told the commandant, "I want to go instead of the man who was selected. He has a wife and family. I am alone. I am a Catholic priest." The priest also contended that he was elderly. Mr Gajowniczek said, "Father Kolbe was then 47". Mr Gajowniczek was 41. The commandant agreed to the switch.*

*In the underground cell, Fr Kolbe sought to console the other condemned men, leading them in prayers and hymns, while awaiting their death by starvation in the hunger bunker. After ten days, on 14 August 1941, Fr Kolbe and three others remained alive. Then a German doctor came and killed them with injections of carbolic acid!*

*Fr Kolbe was beatified in 1971 and in 1982, Pope John Paul II proclaimed 'Fr Kolbe a saint' in the Roman Catholic Church.*

In this true story, Fr Kolbe dying in the place of Gajowniczek, is a remarkable Christian example of 'ransom price' paid by one man to free another. The ransom price paid by the Son of God is of infinitely greater value, as it is able to save the entire human race.

Jesus commands us to take up our cross and follow him. Above is a picture of Simon of Cyrene helping Jesus to carry the cross.

One of the most important teachings of Jesus is that we follow his example and accept and carry the crosses in life. The cross or burden we carry is different for each person. It may be coping with the permanent loss of a loved one, facing a long jail sentence, having cancer or other long-standing illness, such as kidney disease or having to deal with betrayal by someone who was close to you, having a child with disabilities; the list can be endless.

Jesus accepted the cross graciously. He was condemned although they found no fault with him and he was without sin (1 John 3:5 You know that He appeared in order to take away sins; and in Him, there is no sin). When we accept the cross or crosses in our lives, we are sharing in the suffering of Christ and become worthy to share his glory. Romans 8:17 says, "If indeed we share in his sufferings in order that we may also share in his glory."

Like Simon of Cyrene, we are expected to carry each other's burdens and therefore become a blessing to others. In Galatians 6:2, we read: "Carry each other's burdens, and in this way, you will fulfil the law of Christ."

Punch line: On the Cross hangs the love of God!

**Let us pray**: Lord, we pray that you give us the grace to accept the unchangeable situations in our lives and the grace to accept and tolerate others (Romans 15:7). May we imitate Christ and become salt and light in this world that is thirsting for the love of God. Amen

---

CCC 618 The cross is the unique sacrifice of Christ, the "one mediator between God and men". But because in his incarnate divine person he has in some way united himself to every man, "the possibility of being made partners, in a way known to God, in the paschal mystery" is offered to all men. He calls his disciples to "take up [their] cross and follow [him]", for "Christ also suffered for [us], leaving [us] an example so that [we] should follow in his steps."

Apart from the cross there is no other ladder by which we may get to heaven.

---

# Jesus Gives Us His Mother

Today is the feast of 'the Assumption', when we celebrate the teaching of the Holy Catholic Church that Mary, the Mother of Jesus, was taken up to heaven both body and soul. She is our Universal Queen Mother, given to all humanity by Jesus, at the foot of the cross just before his death. In John 19:27, Jesus said to John, "Here is your mother and take her to your home."

Let me give you a message about the power of the Holy Rosary.

Yes indeed, Mary the Mother of God, is praying with us when we pray the Holy Rosary. The Holy Rosary is an absolutely 'one hundred percent Jesus-centred prayer' in which we proclaim the scripture verses from 'Luke 1:28-45'. The Hail Mary is the most powerful scriptural prayer that brings out 'the Good News of the Incarnation, that the Son of God took human flesh' as these are 'the words of Father God' sent to Mary through the Archangel Gabriel! This was the message awaited by the chosen people, Israel, for many centuries!

I want to tell you a true story to show the power of the Holy Rosary and to encourage all to pray the Rosary daily.

*The sixth of August 1945 (World War II) was the darkest day of the twentieth century. At 8:15 am, Fr Schiffer, a Jesuit priest, in Our Lady's Church of the Assumption, had finished celebrating Mass and sat down for breakfast. He sliced a piece of grapefruit when he saw a bright flash of light. This is how Fr Schiffer described it "suddenly a terrific explosion filled the air with a bursting thunder stroke. An invisible force lifted me from the chair, hurled me through the air, shook me, battered me, whirled me round and round like a leaf in a gust of autumn wind."*

*The American B-29 aircraft Enola Gay dropped the first atomic bomb (Little Boy) on Hiroshima in Japan. More than 100,000 people were killed instantly and thousands more died months later from the effects of radiation. However, Our Lady's Church of the Assumption and Fr Schiffer and 7 other priests survived. Nine days later on 15 August, on the feast of the Assumption, the US forces were ordered to ceasefire.*

*After the explosion the next thing he remembered, he opened his eyes, and he was lying on the ground. He looked around; there was NOTHING: the railway station and the buildings in all surrounding areas were levelled to the ground. The only harm to him was that he could feel a few pieces of glass in the back of his neck. After the conquest, it was explained to Fr Schiffer that his body would begin to deteriorate because of the radiation. To the doctors' amazement, Fr Schiffer and the other priests had no radiation ill effects from the bomb throughout their lives.*

*When asked to account for this incredible situation, in which he and his companions were spared, Fr Schiffer said: "We believe that we survived because we were living the message of Fatima. We lived and prayed the Rosary daily in that home." He feels that they "received a protective shield" from the Blessed Mother, which protected them from radiation ill effects. The same protective shield was given to the brothers who prayed the Rosary daily in a Franciscan Friary in Nagasaki, which was also bombed (Fat Man) three days later!*

My dear friends, the Word of God is described as 'the Sword of the Spirit' (Ephesians 6:17) in the Bible. We Catholics are the most blessed people on the face of the Earth, because we have this great armour of the Holy Spirit—the Holy Rosary. It is a divine sword and a divine shield, against the Enemy, the Devil and the disasters, which happen as a consequence of living in a fallen world, like the current pandemic.

My message to you today is to take up the Rosary and pray it daily and unleash its power into your lives. Acknowledge the great gift of Mary, as our Universal Mother, by praying the Rosary and become Her Majesty's People

(HMP) with full access to the throne room of our Lord God Almighty.

CCC 495 Called in the Gospels "the mother of Jesus", Mary is acclaimed by Elizabeth, at the prompting of the Spirit and even before the birth of her son, as "the mother of my Lord". In fact, the One whom she conceived as man by the Holy Spirit, who truly became her Son according to the flesh, was none other than the Father's eternal Son, the second person of the Holy Trinity. Hence the Church confesses that Mary is truly "Mother of God" (Theotokos).

Punch line: The Mother of God proclaims her Son divine!

**Let us pray**: Lord, grant us the grace to accept Mary, as our Universal Heavenly Mother, given to us at the foot of the cross by your Son Jesus Christ (John 19:27). May we understand the power of intercession, given to her in the role of Queen Mother, as in the Kingdom of David. Amen.

# A Call to be Holy

On Palm Sunday, we remember the famous event in the life of Jesus when he entered the Temple in Jerusalem riding on a donkey. This was predicted by the prophet Zechariah hundreds of years before Christ. Jesus fulfilled more than 300 prophecies about himself, and this was one of them! The people hailed Jesus as the Messiah and welcomed him with palm branches (Matthew 21:1-9).

When Jesus entered the temple, he was very angry when he saw people using the temple for buying and selling things because it was God's House and a House of Prayer (Matthew 21:12-14). We assemble in a church, or chapel, to raise our hearts to God, not for leisure or as a pastime! Like this Temple in Jerusalem, our Chapel in Her Majesty's Prison, is a House of Prayer that should be respected by good behaviour.

But the most important point which all should understand and know about the temple, is that our body is now the Temple of the Holy Spirit. St Stephen and then St Paul said, 'how can God be contained or live in a man-made temple' because he's so very BIG, GREAT AND MIGHTY! So, they say that God does not live in man-made temples but rather in our bodies, in our hearts. St Paul says in 1 Corinthians 3:16, 'Surely you know that you are God's temple and that God's Spirit lives in you.' Again in 1 Corinthians 6:19, St Paul writes 'Don't you know that your body is the temple of the

Holy Spirit, who lives in you and who was given to you by God'?

Reciting these Bible verses is very powerful to overcome addictive behaviours. My own late father was a chain smoker whilst having a strong Christian faith. When he heard this verse 'your body is a temple of the Holy Spirit', he realised that his body should be kept 'holy'. He made a firm decision to stop smoking, and for the last nearly 25 years of his life, he never smoked another cigar! Both his faith and his health improved, and his heart disease remained stable for many years.

So, think about these two verses, it is very powerful to help you overcome addictions (nicotine is as addictive as heroin or cocaine) and also habitual sinful behaviour and attitudes like anger, hatred and sexual immorality, to name a few. The Lord says in 1 Peter 1:16, "Be holy because I am holy."

My dear friends let us together do our best to say 'no' to temptation and 'yes' to Jesus every day. We are called to purify ourselves because our Lord Jesus Christ paid a 'VERY

BIG PRICE' to save us from our sins, so that we can have fellowship with God. In the Book of Acts 20:28, St Paul says that actually, 'we were bought with God's own blood meaning the blood of his Son Jesus Christ'.

Punch line: Holiness sets us apart for God!

**Let us pray**: —Dear Jesus, I bring myself into your presence and ask you for mercy for the times I sinned against you by misusing my body. I understand that my body is special and holy and meant to be a temple for the Holy Spirit to reside. Please cleanse this temple of my body, so that I can renew the gift of the Holy Spirit within me. Dear Lord, wash me with your precious blood and fill me with your Holy Spirit and help me to overcome all my bad habits.

I thank and praise you Lord for hearing my prayer. Amen.

---

CCC 364 The human body shares in the dignity of "the image of God": it is a human body precisely because it is animated by a spiritual soul, and it is the whole human person that is intended to become, in the body of Christ, a temple of the Spirit.

---

# Do Not Be Afraid

The main theme in this reflection is about our God who cares for us and knows us very closely. There are three points I will elaborate on:

1. The Lord is at my side.
2. Do not be afraid.
3. The abundant free gift of Jesus Christ.

It is so reassuring to be aware that the Lord is at our side as a mighty hero! There are many passages in the Bible that talk about, or allude to, the loving and caring nature of God. Isn't it amazing that every hair on our head has been counted by God? God is very concerned even when a sparrow falls to the ground and the Bible says that 'you are worth more than many sparrows!' (Matt 10:26-31).

In 1 Peter 5:7, we are advised to cast all our anxieties and worries on to him because he cares for you. Isaiah 43:4-5 says, 'you are precious to me … do not be afraid for I am with you'. One of the most powerful verses is Isaiah 49:16 in which God says, 'I have carved you in the palm of my hands'.

Yes, my friends, he has written your name in the palm of his hands; basically, in today's language, it means God has 'tattooed your name on his hands'! You are always before his eyes. In the book of Psalms, he says that 'you are the apple of my eye' (Psalm 17:8).

It is very clear from the Bible that God cares for us much more than we can imagine. That is why St Paul says, 'if God is for us who can be against us' (Romans 8:31). Because he is for us, God repeatedly says, 'do not be afraid' about anything in this world or what people can do to you. The command from God 'do not be afraid' appears 365 times in the Bible— every day he is telling you do not be afraid!

Instead, the Bible warns us 'to fear only God' because all power and authority belongs to God, and it is to him that we belong—body, mind and spirit. Today, he is telling us that the salvation of our soul is the most important thing in life, and this salvation can be given or won for you by the Lord himself.

This brings us to the final point—the 'abundant free gift of Jesus Christ'. It is only in Jesus Christ that we get forgiveness for our sins. According to God's law, we read in Hebrews 9:22 'without the shedding of blood there is no forgiveness of sins'.

Throughout the Old Testament, God promised to send his Son Jesus to die for our sins. We read in Isaiah 53:5: 'he was pierced for our transgressions; he was crushed for our iniquities; the punishment that brought peace was upon him and by his wounds we are healed'. The chosen people of God repeatedly broke the Ten Commandments.

So, when Jesus died on the cross shedding his blood for us, it was a sacrifice in which 'God himself in Christ was reconciling the world to himself' (2 Corinthians 5:19). St Peter preached that 'Salvation is found in no one else, for there is no other name under heaven given to men by which we must be saved' (Acts 4:12).

The basic need of mankind is forgiveness for our sins. All Christians should be familiar with the Scripture in Romans 3:23, 'for all have sinned and fall short of the glory of God and are justified freely by his grace through the redemption that came by Christ Jesus'. The related Bible verse is Romans 6:23 'for the wages of sin is death, but the gift of God is eternal life in Christ Jesus our Lord'.

I have shared with you today some of the very important or key verses. It will be a worthwhile exercise to read these scriptures frequently. As you read the Word of God more and more, you will find peace and joy replace anxiety, worry and depression in your hearts. Make it a point to read Bible verses daily, either from the Bible or from other books or sources.

The power in the above verses can become perceptible in our lives only if it is prayed with implicit trust in the works of Our Lord Jesus, because it is only in and through Christ that God has shown the world his true image and character as a God of Love. God in Christ on the cross is a clear demonstration of His unfathomable love for us. In Psalm

125:1, we read that 'those who trust in the Lord are like Mount Zion, they shall never be shaken'.

The greatest claim of Christianity, originally and perpetually proclaimed by the One Holy Catholic and Apostolic Church, is that God visited us, in Christ Jesus and he continues to live here on earth, in and through the power of the Holy Spirit to dwell among us and remain with us always.

Punch line: Perfect love conquers fear!

**Let us pray**: O Lord our God, we thank you for the free gift of your beloved Son our Lord Jesus Christ, in whom we have forgiveness of our sins. We believe that there is no condemnation for us in Christ Jesus (Romans 8:1). Lord, grant us the grace to know that you are by our side always, in all situations and circumstances, and that you love us and care for us much more than we can imagine. Pour your love into our hearts, take away all the fears and anxieties from us and help us to obey the command you give us every day— 'DO NOT BE AFRAID'.

---

CCC 1808 Fortitude is the moral virtue that ensures firmness in difficulties and constancy in the pursuit of the good. It strengthens the resolve to resist temptations and to overcome obstacles in the moral life. The virtue of fortitude enables one to conquer fear, even fear of death, and to face trials and persecutions. It disposes one even to renounce and sacrifice his life in defence of a just cause. "The Lord is my strength and my song." "In the world you have tribulation; but be of good cheer, I have overcome the world."

---

# Jesus Forgives

The message today is on FORGIVENESS. The joy and peace of Christian life cannot be fully experienced if we continue to keep hatred, resentment, grudges or anger against those who hurt or injured us in our hearts. When we keep anger against another, harbouring unforgiveness, it becomes a block to answered prayer (Isaiah 59:1-2).

Here is a true story to help us understand the power and amazing love of God present and flowing into our lives, when we forgive the person or people who have injured us.

Corrie Ten Boom is a Christian preacher who had in the past spent time in the concentration camp in Auschwitz. Below is her story, in her own words, when God called her to forgive her cruel guard in the concentration camp whom she met many years later at a preaching appointment:

*It was in a church in Munich where I was speaking in 1947 that I saw him—a balding heavyset man in a grey overcoat, a brown felt hat clutched between his hands. One moment, I saw the overcoat and the brown hat, the next, a blue uniform and a visor cap with its skull and crossbones.*

*Memories of the concentration camp came back with a rush: the huge room with its harsh overhead lights, the pathetic pile of dresses and shoes in the centre of the floor, the shame of walking naked past this man. I could see my sister's frail form ahead of me, ribs sharp beneath the parchment of skin.*

Betsie and I had been arrested for concealing Jews in our home during the Nazi occupation of Holland.

This man had been a guard at Ravensbruck concentration camp where we were sent. Now he was in front of me, hand thrust out: "A fine message, fraulein! How good it is to know that, as you say, all our sins are at the bottom of the sea!"

It was the first time since my release that I had been face to face with one of my captors and my blood seemed to freeze.

"You mentioned Ravensbruck in your talk," he was saying. "I was a guard there. But since that time," he went on, "I have become a Christian. I know that God has forgiven me for the cruel things I did there, but I would like to hear it from your lips as well. Fraulein"—again the hand came out— "will you forgive me?" And I stood there—and could not. Betsie had died in that place—could he erase her slow terrible death simply for asking?

It could not have been many seconds that he stood there, hand held out, but to me, it seemed hours as I wrestled with the most difficult thing I had ever had to do. For I had to do it—I knew that. The message that God forgives has a prior condition: that we forgive those who have injured us. "If you do not forgive men their trespasses," Jesus says, "neither will your Father in Heaven forgive your trespasses." Still, I stood there with the "coldness clutching my heart." But forgiveness is an act of the will, and the will can function regardless of the temperature of the heart. "Jesus, help me!" I prayed silently. "I can lift my hand. I can do that much. You supply the feeling."

And so woodenly, mechanically, I thrust my hand into the one stretched out to me. And, as I did, an incredible thing took place. 'The current started in my shoulder, raced down my *arm, sprang into our joined hands. And then this healing warmth seemed to flood my whole being, bringing tears to my eyes'.*

*"I forgive you, brother!" I cried. "With all my heart!"*

*For a long moment, we grasped each other's hands, the former guard and former prisoner. I had never known God's love as intensely as I did then.*

forgiveness

Forgiveness is one of the seven keys in The Lord's Prayer—Our Father—to unlock the gates of Heaven in our lives.

Punch line: To err is human, to forgive is divine!

**Let us pray**: Dear Lord, as we heard your teaching on the paramount need for us to forgive others, we ask you to give us the grace to love our neighbour, our enemies and those who have hurt us with the forgiving love of God.

I believe that through forgiveness I free my heart and I open my heart to the floodgates of Heaven and an outpouring of your Holy Spirit into my life. Amen.

---

CCC 2843 Thus the Lord's words on forgiveness, the love that loves to the end, become a living reality. The parable of the merciless servant, which crowns the Lord's teaching on ecclesial communion, ends with these words: "So also my heavenly Father will do to every one of you, if you do not forgive your brother from your heart." It is there, in fact, "in the depths of the heart," that everything is bound and loosed. It is not in our power not to feel or to forget an offence; but the heart that offers itself to the Holy Spirit turns injury into compassion and purifies the memory in transforming the hurt into intercession.

# Receive the Holy Spirit

Today, we reflect on the importance of:

1. Opening our hearts to the Word of God and receiving the Holy Spirit.
2. Loving God by keeping the Ten Commandments.

The Holy Spirit is the third person of the Holy Trinity, and it is impossible to live a good Christian life without the Holy Spirit. We have all received the Holy Spirit, especially through baptism, and the Spirit of God was poured into our hearts (Romans 5:5). When Jesus appeared to his disciples through the locked room, after his rising from the dead, Jesus breathed on them and said to them, "Receive the Holy Spirit" (John 20:19,22) The Holy Spirit is the power source, to help us keep our faith and lead a life of prayer. It is the fuel and fire for our Christian journey. Therefore, we need to put effort into re-filling and re-kindling ourselves with the power of the Holy Spirit. The Book of Acts in the Bible is the book about the action, power and work of the Holy Spirit. Whenever the apostles of Jesus spoke the Word of God and laid their hands on people, there was an outpouring of the Holy Spirit.

The Holy Spirit was given to all people without discrimination of race, religion or gender. In my opinion, the Holy Spirit should be the one chairing all the Equality and Diversity Meetings in our organisations! St Paul said in his letter to the Ephesians (Eph 5:18), "Do not be drunk with wine but be filled with the Holy Spirit." In his letter to Timothy (2 Tim 1:7), St Paul said, "the Spirit of God fills us with power, love and self-control".

My personal testimony is about my experience when I had been for a five days Retreat in January 1993 in India. This was the first time I heard the Word of God preached powerfully. Hearing the Word of God daily for five days had an incredible life-changing effect on my heart. It made me open my heart to receive the Holy Spirit, and when the gifted ministers of the Gospel laid their hands on me, I received the Holy Spirit in a very special way, as I was filled with joy and peace. The Holy Spirit gave me the gift of faith (Ephesians 2:8) and the gift to pray (Romans 8:26).

Through this experience, I developed a strong belief in God, and I received many blessings and marvels in my life. I have learnt that the Holy Spirit is like a dove and we can grieve the Holy Spirit and quench the Holy Spirit (make him sad), when we fall into temptation and commit sin. The Holy Spirit can be kept alive in our hearts by a commitment to daily prayer, striving to obey God's Word, abiding by the teaching of the Catholic Church (making a confession regularly) and being aware of our need for God's mercy in Christ Jesus.

It is only when we are filled with the Holy Spirit that we can truly love God and we show our love for God by keeping or obeying his commandments. Love for God and obedience to God are like the two sides of the same coin—you cannot have one without the other. Love and obedience go hand in hand or rather hand in glove!

Here are the Ten Commandments God gave to Moses (Exodus 20) on Mt Sinai:

1.  I am the Lord your God: you shall not have other gods before me.
2.  You shall not take the name of the Lord your God in vain.
3.  Remember the Lord's Day to keep it holy.
4.  Honour your father and your mother.
5.  You shall not kill.
6.  You shall not commit adultery.
7.  You shall not steal.
8.  You shall not bear false witness (tell lies) against your neighbour.
9.  You shall not covet your neighbour's wife.
10. You shall not covet your neighbour's belongings.

By keeping the Commandments 1-3, we show that we love God, and by keeping the Commandments 4-10, we show that we love our neighbour.

Punch line: Be captured and propelled by the Holy Spirit!

**Let us pray**: God of mercy and compassion, have mercy on us and forgive us our sins, through the blood of Jesus, cleanse us and make us white as wool.

Help us to thirst and pray for the Holy Spirit to once again fill us with the love and power of God. Help us to obey and uphold the Ten Commandments that were given to Moses. Amen

---

CCC 91 All the faithful share in understanding and handing on revealed truth. They have received the anointing of the Holy Spirit, who instructs them and guides them into all truth.

---

# Jesus Calls!

In today's message, the Lord Jesus invites us to come to him and unburden all our pain and difficulties when we find the weight of our problems too heavy to carry alone. Jesus compares the weight of our problems to a yoke. A yoke is a wooden crosspiece that is fastened over the necks of two animals and attached to the plough or cart that they are to pull. Normally, a yoke is very heavy, and it needs two oxen to carry the weight and then to pull the cart attached to it.

Yes, our problems are often heavy like this yoke, and we have to carry and pull them along as we journey through our life. But Jesus offers us a solution to lighten the burden we carry, because he promises that the burden will become light, if we follow him or learn from him about how to live a good God-centred life. This is the only way to find rest for your soul by coming to the heart of Jesus.

Saint Augustine is known for his famous quotation: "you have made us for yourself O Lord and our heart is restless until it finds rest in you." This is one of the great promises of Jesus for those who come to him—rest for your heart and soul. In Matthew 11:28-30, Jesus says "Come to me, all you that are weary and are carrying heavy burdens, and I will give you rest. Take my yoke upon you, and learn from me; for I am gentle and humble in heart, and you will find rest for your souls. For my yoke is easy and my burden is light." In the

Bible, the word 'heart' means 'the very centre of our being', the inner core of our identity as a person.

We human beings have essentially three parts – 'body, mind (soul) and spirit' (1 Thessalonians 5:23). The 'heart is at the centre point' where the body, mind and spirit meet. Therefore, any disorder or disease of the body, mind or spirit can have an adverse effect on the 'heart' making us feel burdened, heavy laden and sad.

It is through the sacraments, prayer, Bible reading and singing hymns and songs that we can come to the Sacred Heart of Jesus. So, whenever we pray, we are meeting with the heart of Jesus. Pope Benedict said that in prayer, 'heart speaks to heart'. Prayer is a communication, a dialogue with Jesus in whom the fullness of God's love is open to man. In prayer, we are actually having free consultation and therapy with the greatest doctor, the greatest counsellor, the greatest advocate and the greatest resettlement officer, the greatest Governor and the greatest chaplain. This is because we carry in our heart all types of medical problems, emotional and mental problems and all the social, financial and family problems.

What happens during prayer is that our heart burdened by numerous problems contacts the heart of Jesus. Once the Lord Jesus starts touching our heart, things are definitely bound to change for the better in our life.

Prayer is the most important activity of our life. The brilliant thing about prayer is that prayer does not necessarily need to be fitted into a regime to complete your activity; there is no need for prison officers to escort you; there is no need for a radio or other safety precautions needed to complete your prayer activity!

Only three things are required— 'faith or trust in Jesus' who is alive and always ready to listen to you. Secondly, a commitment to find time, either morning or evening; or preferably twice daily. Thirdly, personal space, by being on our own either on a chair or on our bed. We should speak to him softly or quietly and spend some time in silence just resting our head on his heart. The heart of Jesus is full of mercy, love and compassion.

Reciting the Rosary and reading the Bible during this time are essential ways of praying that will help us spend more time in prayer. Just like food that we need every day to keep us healthy and alive, we need prayer to keep our soul alive and healthy. Jesus told his disciples to pray every day and all the time. King David who was the most well-known King of Israel prayed seven times a day (Psalm 119:164).

The Catholic Church teaches that we should have both Morning Prayer and Evening Prayer. If you really want to experience the healing power of prayer, it is a must that we spend a good bulk of our daily time providing spiritual food to our soul in prayer!

If you are always busy to pray at least once a day regularly, then it will be impossible to develop a loving relationship with God in Christ Jesus. Only prayer makes our belief, faith and trust in the Lord grow and become strong. The only thing the disciples asked Jesus to teach them was how to pray.

Jesus started his ministry by calling and choosing his cabinet of 12 apostles to follow him. Jesus during his life-time had thousands of disciples who followed him. Through the power of the Holy Spirit in the past 2,000 years, Jesus has called not millions but billions of people to follow him. In John 15:16, Jesus said, "it was not you who chose me but I chose you". We are his Chosen people, a Royal Priesthood and Holy Nation, set apart to proclaim the mighty works of him who pulled us out of darkness into his marvellous light (1 Peter 2:7).

Today Jesus is stretching out his hands, calling you to follow him. If you are ready, say yes and dare to run into his loving arms!

Punch line: Respond to the Outstretched Arm of Love!

**Let us pray**: Lord, give us the grace to respond to your call and to come to you. Give us the gift of prayer so that we may come to know you personally. We unburden our hearts to you. May your Sacred Heart that is a burning furnace of love, touch our hearts so that we may find solace and rest for our souls. Help us to realise that it was you who chose us so that by following you, God's eternal plan for our lives may come to fruition (Jeremiah 29:11).

CCC 459 The Word became flesh to be our model of holiness: "Take my yoke upon you, and learn from me." "I am the way, and the truth, and the life; no one comes to the Father, but by me." On the mountain of the Transfiguration, the Father commands: "Listen to him!" Jesus is the model for the Beatitudes and the norm of the new law: "Love one another as I have loved you." This love implies an effective offering of oneself, after his example.

# Jesus: The Bridegroom

A wedding banquet is a lavish meal given to guests after the wedding ceremony. Whenever invited to a wedding feast, the guests on accepting the invitation, have a responsibility in terms of turning up for the wedding and wearing the right wedding dress code.

My son's wedding banquet was one of the most joyous and memorable days in my life. But the only blemish of the occasion was that one of my close friends did not turn up for the wedding! It made me feel both disappointed and angry!

Secondly, I remember the time I went to a wedding banquet NOT wearing the expected dress code—a black and white suit. I felt like a fish out of water!

The two lessons I learnt from these experiences are, to always be one hundred percent certain of going to the wedding banquet and if you are going to accept such an invitation, make sure you have the right clothes on.

My friend was having a destination wedding for his daughter in another country! The requirement was that all attending should stay at a particular five-star hotel and that gentlemen wore a bow tie! All this was self-funded and would cost about £2,500! I said 'NO' to attending because it required a huge personal investment!

The meaning of today's wedding banquet parable is that God our Father is inviting each one of us, to the Wedding Banquet of His only Son Jesus Christ. There is one difference in this Banquet; we are not mere invitees but 'the bride of Christ'. The Father expects us to say 'YES' to the invitation and to be wearing the dress code for the Heavenly Wedding Banquet (Revelation 19:8-9), even though it requires a huge personal investment!

Accepting the invitation from a Christian point of view means that we accept Jesus Christ as our Saviour and the Wedding Banquet dress we should be wearing is not merely a black and white suit and bow tie but to be washed in the blood of the Lamb (the blood of Jesus) and the colour of our garment should be pure white (Revelation 7:14). The garment we wear stands for our good works washed in the blood of the Lamb! If we depend ONLY on our good works to save us and reject the blood of Jesus, our wedding garments are never going to be pure white! Oh, how we need the blood of Jesus!

In the Book of Revelation, it is clear there will be the grandest and biggest ever Wedding Banquet in Heaven at the end of time, which will be devoid of the drawbacks of an earthly banquet because this will be truly a Heavenly Banquet! I don't know about you, but I certainly want to be one of the esteemed guests—part of the very bride of Christ! My garment will be pure white because it will be washed clean NOT by my good works only BUT by the Blood of Christ who died to save us all!

The garment of self-righteousness has no place in the Kingdom of God! And, for those whose garments have been washed in the blood of Christ, the wedding garment becomes a pure white robe. The white robe is the robe of righteousness in Christ and who then produce the fruits of the Spirit of God—love, joy, peace, patience, kindness, gentleness, goodness, faithfulness and self-control (Galatians 5:22).

Like in the Jewish tradition; the groom (Jesus) and the bride (the chosen people of God) have met when Jesus lived among us 2,000 years ago. The marriage contract is the Salvation plan of the Father (already written in the Bible) and from that moment on, we the bride are engaged to Christ.

But, like in the Jewish tradition, the groom goes back to his house (Jesus has gone back to heaven) to prepare the home for his bride. This may take a long time and the groom (Jesus) will return unannounced when the home is ready! But he expects the bride to be dressed and ready when he, Jesus, the groom returns. Then there will be this long-awaited golden day of the Wedding Feast of the Lamb in Heaven when all invited will come and will be wearing the right dress code!

Punch line: Cleansing power of the Blood of Jesus!

**Let us pray**: Father God, we pray that you wash us in your precious blood of your only begotten Son Jesus Christ, from any spot, stain or wrinkle and fill us with your Holy Spirit. May the Holy Spirit help us live in the righteousness of Christ and that we may spread your love, joy and peace around us to others. Help us to turn the eyes of our heart to look upwards, to participate one day in the Heavenly Wedding feast of the Lamb, promised to each one of us. Amen

CCC 796 The unity of Christ and the Church, head and members of one Body, also implies the distinction of the two within a personal relationship. This aspect is often expressed by the image of bridegroom and bride. The theme of Christ as Bridegroom of the Church was prepared for by the prophets and announced by John the Baptist. The Lord referred to himself as the "bridegroom." The Apostle speaks of the whole Church and of each of the faithful, members of his Body, as a bride "betrothed" to Christ the Lord so as to become but one spirit with him. The Church is the spotless bride of the spotless Lamb. "Christ loved the Church and gave himself up for her, that he might sanctify her." He has joined her with himself in an everlasting covenant and never stops caring for her as for his own body.

# Jesus: The Good Shepherd

The main focus of the readings today is to make us understand that Jesus Christ is the Good Shepherd (John 10:11 – I am the good shepherd). The famous Psalm 23, 'The Lord is my Shepherd', is called 'The Pearl' of all the psalms.

There are two points that I would like to explain.

Firstly, St Peter fervently and unapologetically, in his first preaching appointment, says: save yourselves from this corrupt generation (Acts 2:40) by believing in Jesus as your Saviour and being filled with the Holy Spirit. This is a time to thirst and hunger to receive a fresh outpouring of the Holy Spirit as we approach Pentecost Sunday. The fact is that we cannot live the Christian life without the Holy Spirit because our human nature is weak, and we live in a corrupt world, and it is very easy to be led in the wrong direction.

Secondly, Jesus is the Good Shepherd and cares for his sheep. In John 10:11, we read 'I am the good shepherd. The good shepherd lays down his life for the sheep'.

Of all the animals, God compares human behaviour to that of sheep. The sheep depend completely on the shepherd on a daily basis, and the shepherd loves his sheep so much that he is prepared to die for his sheep. King David who was a shepherd before he became a King, has killed a lion and a bear with his bare hands to protect his sheep. The sheep depend on the shepherd and without a shepherd, they go astray and are lost.

Another speciality of sheep is that they recognise only the voice of their shepherd and not the voice of any stranger who calls them (John 10:5 – "they do not know the voice of strangers"). We know very well that we recognise the voice of those very close to us.

In my previous job, I had a secretary, and I often dictate my letters onto a dictaphone, which records my voice. My secretary then types the letters by replaying my voice on a dictaphone player and listening to my voice using headphones. So now she can hear my voice very clear and very loud because all other sounds are shut out by the headphones. This is something that she had to do every day, and I had worked in that job for more than 10 years. Through this experience of hearing my voice every day for more than 10 years through headphones, she learnt to recognise my voice very well. Because she is so familiar with my voice, she is able to recognise my voice even if there are other background voices or noises.

Therefore, we must get used to listening to the voice of Jesus. There is only one way; that is spend personal prayer time with Jesus every day, and this should be as important as the time you give to eat your main meal of the day. If you make this a daily commitment, you will learn to hear his voice and come to know his voice. This is important because there are so many voices and noises around us saying different things to us and may be misleading us. But if you know Jesus and his voice, he will 'lead you to green pastures and make you rest beside quiet streams of water' (Psalm 23:2).

The lockdown period and similar periods like off days, is the best and most ideal time to develop a personal relationship with Jesus. Find a suitable time in the day or night when your mind is calm and spend at least 30 minutes with Jesus.

The main message of the Bible is that Jesus is the Son of God and he has repeatedly said that he is the way to the Father and he said that if we know him then we know the Father. Jesus says, 'I am the gate' (John 10:9) and anyone who enters through me is safe.

So, like obedient sheep in a flock who know the voice of their shepherd, let us also learn to hear the voice of Jesus by making a decision today to find daily personal prayer time with him for at least 30 minutes. The promise is that 'you will have life and life to the full' (John 10:10).

Punch line: Hear His Master's Voice

**Let us pray**: Lord Jesus, I thank you for being with me in my journey of life. Thank you for protecting me from the coronavirus. I ask you today that you send the Holy Spirit on me to help me pray daily in my weakness (Romans 8:26). Holy Spirit, please come into my heart and give me the desire and the commitment to spend daily personal time with Jesus. Lord, I believe you are the gate, and in you, I have life to the full. Jesus, my Good Shepherd, protect me and save me from people and circumstances that can cause me harm. Jesus, I believe in you. Jesus, I trust in you. Amen.

CCC 764 'This Kingdom shines out before men in the word, in the works and in the presence of Christ." To welcome Jesus' word is to welcome "the Kingdom itself." The seed and beginning of the Kingdom are the "little flock" of those whom Jesus came to gather around him, the flock whose shepherd he is. They form Jesus' true family. To those whom he thus gathered around him, he taught a new "way of acting" and a prayer of their own.

# Jesus in the Holy Eucharist

Today is the feast of 'Corpus Christi', which means 'Body and Blood of Christ'. This is a very Catholic teaching, and it originates from the words of Jesus in today's Gospel reading. Jesus calls himself the living bread (John 6:51) or in other words the heavenly manna. Jesus does not stop with this teaching but goes on to say that the living bread is his flesh (John 6:53-56) and that anyone who eats his flesh and drinks his blood will have eternal life (John 6:54).

The Early Christian Church had this belief that the bread that Jesus broke and the wine that Jesus blessed (Matthew 26:26-29) at the Last Supper were literally his very body and blood. This Sacrament of the Holy Eucharist started by Jesus has been practiced by the presbyters or the priests in the Catholic Church for the past 2,000 years.

In the Holy Mass, when the priest blesses the bread and wine, a great miracle happens; the bread and wine are changed into the Body and Blood of Christ. This is known as *transubstantiation*, and the Holy Eucharist becomes the real presence of Jesus. This Catholic Christian teaching is different from most Protestant teaching. There is a gradual drift and dilution of the belief in the real presence of Christ in the Eucharist, especially in the non-denominational evangelical churches.

The important point to keep in mind is that in Holy Communion during the Holy Mass, it is the real body and blood of Jesus that we eat and drink. It is a very special, holy, sacred time when we have a very close communion with the Lord. Therefore, it is always important to prepare our hearts spiritually before receiving the Holy Communion. Ask the Lord pardon for our sins so that our hearts are clean and open for Jesus to come into our hearts.

*In the eighth century, when a monk (priest) was celebrating Holy Mass, he doubted the belief that the 'bread and wine' become the 'body and blood of Jesus'. As this monk was saying the Consecration Prayer (blessing) over the bread and wine, the priest saw the bread change into living flesh and the wine change into blood, which coagulated (clotted) into five globules (five parts), irregular and differing in shape and size. This happened in Lanciano in Italy and is known as the Eucharistic Miracle of Lanciano.*

*They found that the five globules were of different sizes and shapes, but the weight of one globule (one part) was the same weight as the five globules weighed together (called the miracle of weights). The specimens (sample) from this miracle were examined in the laboratory and found to be the same as human heart muscle tissue and the blood group was AB positive group. They found no preservatives, and the relics are until today kept in the Church of St Francis at Lanciano in Italy.*

The Holy Eucharist for Catholic Christians is believed to be 'the Sacrament of Sacraments'. Holy Communion time is a very extraordinary moment in our prayer life that we human beings on earth actually 'Passover' from earth to heaven. If we fully understand the holiness of this sacrament, Holy Communion gives us a foretaste of heaven. In the Journey Home TV programme telecast by EWTN network, we hear amazing stories of how Protestants become Catholic when they understand the real presence of Jesus Christ in the Holy Eucharist.

In the Old Testament, God gave the Israelites manna from heaven daily, and this food from heaven, gave them strength to survive and sustain them when they were in the wilderness for 40 years before they reached the Promised Land. The manna helped them in their Passover journey from slavery in Egypt to the freedom of the Promised Land in Canaan (in Israel).

How much more will we be sustained by the Body and Blood of Christ in our earthly journey from slavery to sin to the freedom of the peace, love and joy of the Kingdom of God in the Holy Eucharist!

I want to tell you about an astronaut on Apollo 11, who was a man of great faith. Did you know that the second person to step foot on the moon did something marvellous? It has been made public that Buzz Aldrin celebrated the Lord's Supper, upon landing on the moon in the Eagle LM.

*He gave thanks to God for the event of this historic achievement of man. Aldrin opened the little plastic package which contained the bread and wine. He poured wine into a chalice and in the 1/6 gravity of the moon, the wine slowly curled up the side of the cup.*

*He read the Scripture 'I am the vine you are the branches, whoever abides in me will bring forth much fruit'.*

*He ate the tiny host and swallowed the wine and gave thanks to God for the intelligence and the Spirit that had brought two pilots to the Sea of Tranquillity.*

*On returning to earth, he read Psalm 8 'When I look at your heavens, the work of your fingers, the moon and the stars that you have established...'*

*The first act on the moon was a communion service and first food and drink consumed on the moon were the communion elements.* God is great. Halleluia!

Punch line: The Host of hosts is the greatest love story!

**Let us pray**: Lord Our God, we thank you for this great gift of the Holy Eucharist and your real presence as body, blood, soul and divinity in the Eucharist. Grant us the realisation of the importance of the holiness of our lives, in order to participate fully in Holy Communion, opening our hearts to experience joy, peace and love of the Kingdom of God in this Heavenly Banquet. Amen.

1324 The Eucharist is "the source and summit of the Christian life." "The other sacraments, and indeed all ecclesiastical ministries and works of the apostolate, are bound up with the Eucharist and are oriented toward it. For in the blessed Eucharist is contained the whole spiritual good of the Church, namely Christ himself, our Pasch."

# Jesus – the Key

Today the Lord is speaking to us about the importance of doors and keys in our life. We are all part of a community who either live or work in a prison, and nothing is more obvious, routine and of great importance, than an emphasis on doors and keys. The penalty for negligence in leaving a door unlocked in prison is immediate dismissal! New recruits are not given immediate access to keys and are only given access to prison keys after rigorous training. Therefore, the key used to lock or unlock a door is as vital as the door itself.

The key is not only a symbol of authority, access and freedom, but also responsibility. I remember the time I first started working in prison and did not have access to keys. I was dependent on the goodness of other chaplains to get me around the prison as well as in and out of the prison premises. It was impossible to do my job without the keys! In the world of computers, the key to open a window or a document is the password.

The Bible teaches us that this amazingly powerful key or password to unlock doors, which give us entry or access to heavenly blessings in this life and eventually life everlasting, is the name of JESUS. This is clear from the following Bible verses:

Colossians 2:2-3: "In this way they will know God's secret, which is Christ himself. He is the key that opens all the hidden treasures of God's wisdom and knowledge".

Revelation 3:7: "He has the key that belonged to David and when he opens a door, no one can close it and when he closes it, no one can open it".

Jesus said to St Peter, the first Pope, in Matthew 16:19, "I will give you the keys of the Kingdom of heaven; what you prohibit on earth will be prohibited in heaven, and what you permit on earth will be permitted in heaven". It was here that Jesus handed over a share in his divine authority to St Peter and the Church.

The keys of the Kingdom or the key to the Kingdom is JESUS himself. The hallmark of the ministry and teaching of Jesus was his divine or Godly authority. He always pointed to himself as "the Way, the Truth and the Life" (John 14:6) and said "whoever has seen me has seen the Father" (John 14:9).

The reason that St Peter was given the awesome authority to decide about prohibiting or permitting things on earth by being given the keys to the Kingdom, was because he knew the key; Peter knew Jesus, and the key is the statement of belief: 'Jesus, you are the Messiah, the Son of the living God' (Matthew 16:16).

The question before each one of us today is: Do we know Jesus? Do we know him personally as the God who saves and as the Son of the living God? We will come to know him more and more as we purify our lives and align our thoughts, words and deeds, to the teaching of Jesus and the words of life that fell from his divine lips (John 6:63: my words are spirit and they are life).

God has a plan for each of our lives (Jeremiah 29:11). As we communicate with God through prayer, this great blueprint of our lives will unfold before us step by step. I had a plan to work as a Prison Chaplain, and I prayed about this plan for more than a year. I prayed, Lord Jesus you hold the key to my destiny; close the door to my previous job and open the door to chaplaincy. Yes, he answered my prayer at the appropriate time by opening prison doors, so that I may proclaim Christ here. Jesus can do the same for you.

Therefore, dear friends, the password to open doors in your life and to enter the pearly gates of Heaven is 'Jesus is Lord'! This is the password of the Father that was kept secret from ancient of days and has 'now been revealed' into the public domain. It is universal, free and easy to remember. Both lowercase and / or capitals will work, and spacing is allowed because of current social distancing rules in COVID times!

Punch line: 'Jesus is Lord' password has now gone viral!

**Let us pray**: Heavenly Father, send us your Holy Spirit as a Revelation enabling us to believe that the name of your Son Jesus Christ is the secret key to unlock the pearly gates of Heaven. Amen.

---

CCC 455 The title "Lord" indicates divine sovereignty. To confess or invoke Jesus as Lord is to believe in his divinity. "No one can say 'Jesus is Lord' except by the Holy Spirit'" (1 Cor 12:3)

# Jesus – the Friend of Prisoners

The Bible says that Jesus loves prisoners! There are many verses in the Bible about the Lord being present among us in the person of prisoners. In Matthew 25:36, Jesus says, "I was in prison and you came to visit me". The one I frequently quote is Psalm 146:7: "The Lord sets prisoners free".

In my opinion, every prison is a place chosen by the Lord for your spiritual renewal—to turn to God by renouncing all your previous sins and making a decision to live an upright life with integrity. This task is not easy, but the Bible says in Philippians 4:13, "I can do all things through Christ who strengthens me".

Like in the parable told by Jesus in the Gospel today, there are many people who are saying 'NO' to God by their chaotic lifestyle, but later, when they experience the love of God in Christ Jesus, they are able to say a big 'YES' to God. Jesus was very critical of so-called self-righteous people like the Pharisees, priests and teachers of the law. This is because it is only the humble and those who associate with the lowly are open to God's grace. We read in Romans 12:16: 'Live in harmony with each other. Don't be too proud not to enjoy the company of ordinary people. And don't think you know it all'.

Jesus himself left his divine status and took our human form (Philippians 2:7). But he remained both God and man.

Jesus said in Mark 2:17, "I have not come to call the righteous but sinners". Today, we heard Jesus say that the tax collectors and prostitutes will make their way to the Kingdom of God before the self-righteous who follow the law, because in the process, they overlook divine attributes like kindness and compassion, for the outcasts and marginalised people.

Here is the true story of a prisoner in UK jails who is now a well-known and popular witness to the work of Jesus Christ, in our day and age, to turn a life around from crime and punishment to freedom and grace.

*Shane Taylor was considered one of the most dangerous men in the UK prison system. Originally jailed for attempted murder, he had his sentence extended by four years when he attacked a prison officer with broken glass, setting off a riot.*

*He was put in a segregation unit inside a maximum-security prison. He was given his food through a hatch. His door was not opened unless there were six officers armed with riot shields waiting outside.*

*Whilst he was resident in the maximum-security prison, he was invited to 'an Alpha course' which is a basic Christian Initiation Course. During the course, he prayed, "Jesus Christ, I know you died on the cross for me. I hate who I am, who I've become. Please forgive me and come into my life." At that moment, he was filled with the Holy Spirit. Everything changed overnight. He said, "I knew God existed, I knew Jesus had touched me and I was going to live for him forever."*

*His behaviour changed so much that he went from living in total segregation to getting a trusted job in the prison chaplaincy. Whilst still in prison, he started sending money to a charity in Africa. He prayed for the prison officers and for his enemies, and when he came out of prison, he got involved* in a church. He met a girl called Sam, who had also had a tough life and had been involved with drugs and criminal activity. She also came to faith in Jesus. Now, they are married and have four children. Talking to Shane now, it is hard to imagine that he is the same person who terrified so many people in his past.

He says, "Jesus has shown me how to love and how to forgive. He has saved me. He has forgiven me for what I have done. He has turned my life around."

Here are the lyrics of a song written by another prisoner after being transformed through the deepening of his faith in Christ as his Saviour:

*Turn to God, turn to God*
*Oh my God I turn to you*
*Through your Son Jesus Christ*
*I myself turn to you*
*Send upon me your Holy Spirit*
*That I may spread your Word*
*Turn to God, turn to God*
*Oh my God I turn to you*
*Jesus Christ our Saviour*
*Showed me the path to you*
*On my journey I found mercy*
*So now I turn to you*
*Turn to God, turn to God*
*Oh, my God, I have turned to you!*
*Amen! Amen! Amen!*

"The King will reply, 'I tell you the truth, whatever you did for one of the least of these brothers of mine, you did for me.' Matthew 25:40.

Punch line: Jesus the Psychiatrist, mending souls!

**Let us pray**: Lord, I pray that all prisoners are given the grace to pray the prayer that Shane Taylor prayed: "Jesus Christ, I know you died on the cross for me. I hate who I am, who I've become. Please forgive me and come into my life."

May all prisoners be filled with the Holy Spirit to lead an abundant life that Jesus promised us (John 10:10). Amen.

827 "Christ, 'holy, innocent, and undefiled,' knew nothing of sin, but came only to expiate the sins of the people. The Church, however, clasping sinners to her bosom, at once holy and always in need of purification, follows constantly the path of penance and renewal." All members of the Church, including her ministers, must acknowledge that they are sinners. In everyone, the weeds of sin will still be mixed with the good wheat of the Gospel until the end of time. Hence the Church gathers sinners already caught up in Christ's salvation but still on the way to holiness.

# Jesus is Lord over Worry

Today I want to focus on the letter of St Paul to the Philippians, emphasising that 'there is no need to worry'.

Worry is defined as 'to think about problems or unpleasant things that might happen in a way that makes you feel unhappy and frightened'. Worry can lead to anxiety and anxiety can lead to fear and mental disorders.

Our common worries can be categorised under seven common problems faced by people—relationships, money, health, job, poor diet, media overload, lack of sleep and finally even where to park!

I have suffered with anxiety symptoms from early childhood, which eventually led me to pursue a career in psychiatry. Over the last 30 years after knowing Jesus and following him, my anxiety has abated a great deal. I must testify here, that I have been 90% healed by the healing love of the Lord, in the inner recesses of my mind.

In the Bible, we find many verses through which the Lord is giving us a command: Do not worry; do not be anxious; do not be afraid.

Here are the important Bible verses we should know and read aloud daily, and it will help us overcome worry in our life:

1) Proverbs 12:25: "Anxiety in a man's heart weighs him down, but a good word makes him glad."
2) 1 Peter 5:7: "Cast all your anxiety on him because he cares for you."
3) Matthew 6:25-26: "Therefore I tell you, do not worry about your life, what you will eat or drink; or about your body, what you will wear. Is not life more than food, and the body more than clothes? Look at the birds of the air; they do not sow or reap or store away in barns, and yet your heavenly Father feeds them."

There are many psychological methods like meditation to help us deal with worry and anxiety but the Holy Scriptures teach us, that the best remedy for worry is restoring our broken relationship with God by turning from our sins and finding time for prayer every day.

I have an allocated prayer time daily; my unloading worry-free time when I present all my worries, anxieties and fears at the feet of Jesus. I have confidence in Jesus Christ, who has conquered the world —he did this when he defeated death (the ultimate enemy of man) by rising from the dead— the glorious Resurrection of Jesus Christ! In John 16:33, Jesus said 'in me you have peace. In the world you face persecution. But take courage; I have conquered the world'!

Slow deep breathing exercise is a recommended way to reduce anxiety. I practice slow breathing and couple it with the Jesus prayer, to help in my anxious worrying moments.

The Jesus Prayer is 'Jesus, Son of the Living God, have mercy on me a poor sinner'. As we learn to say it regularly along with each breath, it can become a continuous prayer throughout the day—Jesus will become part of our breath!

Another prayer exercise that is most powerful and rewarding is to meditate on the Life of Christ by reciting the Holy Rosary. Reciting five decades of the Rosary takes about 20 minutes, but it becomes a source of peace in our lives and in addition a permanent investment for Heaven. St Paul says in 1 Tim 4:8: "physical exercise is of some value but spiritual exercise holds promise for both present life and life to come".

IF YOU HAVE TIME TO WORRY, YOU HAVE TIME TO PRAY.

There are more than 7000 promises offered in the Bible if you do the following:

1) Worry about nothing
2) Pray about everything
3) Thank God in all things
4) Keep your mind on good things
5) Be content in all things and do not compare with others

Prayer and worry are inversely related: the more you pray, the less you worry!

Worry can be unnatural, unhealthy, unreasonable, unhelpful and unnecessary!

Of all God's creatures ONLY, human beings worry! Worry never makes problems smaller but bigger! Worry cannot make you one inch taller or one inch shorter; all worry can do is to make the day worse and add a few more wrinkles to your face!

Punch line: Be worry-free, wrinkle-free!

**Let us pray**: I pray that the Our Lord will bless you and keep you from worry and give you the gift of daily prayer life. Lord our God, give us grace not to worry, but instead to make our supplication and prayers with thanksgiving known to you, so that the peace coming from you, which surpasses understanding, will guard our hearts and minds in Christ Jesus (Philippians 4: 6-7). Amen

---

CCC 2830 "Our bread": The Father who gives us life cannot not but give us the nourishment life requires – all appropriate goods and blessings, both material and spiritual. In the Sermon on the Mount, Jesus insists on the filial trust that cooperates with our Father's providence. He is not inviting us to idleness, but wants to relieve us from nagging worry and preoccupation. Such is the filial surrender of the children of God.

---

# Jesus: The Love of God

Today's Gospel reading emphasises that love should be the driving force of our lives. In 1 John 4:8, the Bible says that 'God is love'. Love is the very image of God, and we the people of God are made in his image.

There are four types of love that we encounter as human beings, and each type of love has its appropriate place in our lives. It is the disregard for this commandment of love that is often at the heart of most of the problems we face.

*Eros* or erotic love is the romantic love between husband and wife, which becomes a joy and blessing whether or not they have children and if they do then it is especially present in their lives.

*Storge* love is the love seen within a family and manifest as the deep affection for our next of kin, shown as concern and help for each other. My sisters and I pray the Holy Rosary together on Zoom weekly, as an expression of our familial love!

*Philia* is the brotherly love shared by friends which is a very deep affection. It is seen as an enduring long-term friendship, especially being there for each other, through times of trial.

Here is an example of storge and philia love shown by one of the prisoners at the funeral of his first cousin who died tragically at a young age. They were both the same age and grew up together.

*Dearest Brother,*

*This is one of the hardest things I have ever had to do.*

*You weren't just my cousin, but you were my brother, my best friend, my mate for 30 years. I have grown from a boy to a man with you. Any hard time we had, I got through with you. It doesn't feel REAL not hearing your voice everyday 'WUAGL CUZZY'—giving me life—being there for me any time of the day. The love I have for you can't be replaced or ever lost. I think of you night and day. I can't cry any more tears.*

*I just keep remembering all our memories, and I can hear you telling me 'It's alright'. Everything I aim for will be in your memory. Any car I have will be the one you wanted—blue lights, neon lights, big speakers!*

*Your life will never leave me, and our memories will never change. My love will only grow stronger. I love and miss you, my brother.*

*Your brother*

*Agape* love is the love of God which is different; it is an unconditional love and gives without expecting anything in return— "Jesus died on the cross for us while we were sinners" (Romans 5:8). Agape love is not merely affection, 'but an act of will, to make a decision to love'—a love as vast as the ocean and reaches the lost, the unloved and the marginalised. St Thomas Aquinas, theologian and Doctor of the Church, defined love as 'willing the good of the other'.

St Mother Teresa of Calcutta is a good example of the agape love of God in action. She heard the voice of Jesus to leave her convent and venture out on the streets of Calcutta, to touch and care for the lepers and the homeless. Here are a few of her famous quotes about love:

- "We do not need guns and bombs to bring peace, we need love and compassion".
- "I have found the paradox, that if you love until it hurts, there can be no more hurt, only more love".
- "Not all of us can do great things. But we can do small things with great love".

**The Four Types of Love in the Bible**

Eros
sensual or romantic love

Storge
familial love

Philia
brotherly love that unites believers

Agape
God's love for humankind

Learn Religions

Punch line: Service – the Language of Love!

**Let us pray**: O God of mercy and compassion, abounding in love, we ask you to pour out your love, into our hearts, to help us be kind and good to each other and make a difference in this world, even to the extent of loving our enemies. We make this prayer through Christ Our Lord. Amen.

CCC 221 But St. John goes even further when he affirms that "God is love": God's very being is love. By sending his only Son and the Spirit of Love in the fullness of time, God has revealed his innermost secret: God himself is an eternal exchange of love, Father, Son and Holy Spirit, and he has destined us to share in that exchange.

God is Love

-1 John 4:16

# Jesus: God in Human Form

The focus of this reflection is on the person of Jesus and the question that all people have to ask themselves is: Who is Jesus? Jesus himself asked the disciples: 'Who do you say I am?' (Matthew 16:15)

In the Gospels written by Matthew, Mark and Luke, the accounts are about what Jesus said and did during his life. It gives us a clear understanding that he was 'fully human'. But the people who saw him and heard him, were puzzled by this amazing character and his mighty miracles and wisdom, in the things he said about love and his attitude to others including our enemies.

The disciples who knew him closely believed that Jesus was not merely a human being but that he was, in fact, the Son of God. In the Gospel of John, Jesus is presented as a person with the very nature of God, and the main focus is on Jesus as the Son of God—'a fully divine Jesus'.

The Christian belief is that Jesus is both fully human and fully divine (100% man and 100% God).

There is a story told of a little girl who was doing a drawing. Her mother asked her, "What are you drawing?"

She replied that she was drawing a picture of God.

The mother was surprised and said, "But no one has seen God?"

The little girl replied, "You will see what he looks like when I have finished!"

She had drawn a face of Jesus! Actually, the little girl was spot on because the Bible says in Colossians 1:15 that: "Jesus is the image (visible likeness) of the invisible God."

There were many great prophets and philosophers and religious leaders who lived in this world such as Socrates, Plato, Buddha etc. But no one has ever pointed to themselves as the gold standard to follow, in order to reach heaven or eternal life. They all pointed to a set of principles or rules to follow in order to reach God.

But, in today's reading, Jesus is the only one who pointed to himself as the gold standard by saying 'I am the Way, the Truth and the Life'. In other words, he was saying that seeing him and following him was the same as following God. He actually was saying that 'I am God in human form, fully divine and fully human'.

Jesus used the word 'I AM' many times, and 'I AM' is the name by which God introduced himself to Moses in the burning bush (Exodus chapter 3). Jesus said, "I am the Resurrection and the life (John 11:25); I am the bread of life (John 6:35); I am the light of the world (John 8:12); I am the gate (John 10:9); I am the Good Shepherd (John 10:11); I am the alpha and the omega (Revelation 1:8). The Hebrew word for 'I am' is 'Yahweh', written originally as 'YHWH' – too holy to be pronounced by human lips!

People say and many other religions say that Jesus was a great prophet and great teacher and that he was not the Son of God. However, the disciples who moved with Jesus closely and knew him intimately were convinced and believed that Jesus was God in human flesh, when he lived on earth.

C.S. Lewis, a great Christian author argues that when we examine the life of Jesus closely, he DID NOT leave open the option that Jesus was merely a great prophet or a great teacher.

The life of Jesus was extraordinary, exemplary and marked by the miraculous. The *Time* magazine rated Jesus as 'the most persistent symbol of purity, selflessness and love in the history of humanity'.

Jesus Christ said and did things that only God could say or do!

C.S. Lewis says there are ONLY three options Jesus Christ left open about himself:

1) He was and is God.
2) He was bad.
3) He was mad.

Lewis is of the opinion, using the deductive analysis method of a detective like Sherlock Holmes, we can confidently conclude that Jesus was neither bad nor mad. This leaves us with only one startling alternative: that Jesus was and is God! In Jesus, God had visited planet earth in human form. Jesus allowed his disciples to call him 'Lord and God' and worship him (John 20:28: Thomas answered him, "My Lord and my God!"). Worship is only meant for God as said in Matthew 4:10: "Worship the Lord your God and serve only him."

### THE WORD MADE FLESH

*In every religion & philosophy,
word remains word - - -
Religion remains a theory
& Philosophy remains a guess...?
But IN Jesus Christ...
the Word is made flesh,
Reality is revealed - - -
God's thought & intent before the
foundations of the world is
concluded in a human life. His
ultimate destiny of THE WORD,
was never a book or an
institution, but the image and
likeness of GOD. . . .
        displayed in man !*

TURBO_RELOADED

There are many other arguments that show that Jesus is the Son of God. So, as good Christians and Catholics, let us hold onto this precious belief, in John 3:16, 'for God so loved the world that he sent his only begotten Son that whosoever believes him may not perish but have everlasting life'.

Punch line: Jesus Christ, fully human, fully divine – the ancient secret revealed!

**Let us pray**: Lord Jesus, we thank you for giving us a strong belief that you are the Son of God.
Be with us, as you promised, through the ups and downs of our journey of life. We pray that many people will turn from their sinful ways and return to you. Jesus, we trust in you. Amen.

CCC 461 Taking up St. John's expression, "The Word became flesh", the Church calls "Incarnation" the fact that the Son of God assumed a human nature in order to accomplish our salvation in it. In a hymn cited by St. Paul, the Church sings the mystery of the Incarnation:

Have this mind among yourselves, which is yours in Christ Jesus, who, though he was in the form of God, did not count equality with God a thing to be grasped, but emptied himself, taking the form of a servant, being born in the likeness of men. And being found in human form he humbled himself and became obedient unto death, even death on a cross.

# Reason-defying faith!

The three main characters in the reflection today are Jesus, Peter and Elijah.

'Elijah' was one of the famous prophets in the Old Testament and had a Christ-like personality, by what he said and did, because he performed miracles, through his unwavering strong faith in the supernatural power of Almighty God. Elijah is known for raising a dead boy to life, ending a drought by praying for rain and bringing fire down from heaven to burn a sacrifice.

The most amazing event in Elijah's life was that he was taken into heaven in a chariot of fire drawn by horses (2 Kings 2:11) and his death has not been recorded in history. Again, like Jesus and Moses, he too had taken a fast for 40 days. Elijah was indeed a very holy prophet, and no wonder that he was taken straight to heaven!

In 1 Kings 19:12-13, an important point to note is that the Lord spoke to Elijah in a soft voice, at a time of sheer silence, when he was standing on a mountain. Jesus went away to the hills to pray for many hours. The lesson for us is to find time and space to pray quietly to God and we will be able to hear him as 'a still small voice' but clear and distinct. Daily personal prayer time is a key factor in developing a relationship with the Lord and to increase our faith in him like the great prophet Elijah.

Peter, the first Pope of the Catholic Church, started his faith journey as a man of little faith, which Jesus refers to in the Gospel reading Matthew 14: 22-33. Here we find that, the key to having a strong faith is to keep our focus on Jesus. Peter was able to walk on the water when he kept his eyes on Jesus. The moment he felt the force of the wind, he took his eyes off Jesus and he began to sink into the water!

When we have to face a storm in our lives and we feel the force of the problem impacting us, there is a good chance that we lose our focus on Jesus. But Jesus is telling us today, do not be afraid but trust in me and do not lose sight of me. Jesus is calling us to look at him, who is the solution for all our problems. If we focus all our energy and time on our problem, then it will appear as an immovable mountain to us. Similarly, if we focus on Jesus in the midst of our problem; it will gradually diminish in size, and Jesus will grow bigger in our mind, making us feel stronger than the problem.

Put your faith in Jesus and he will help you weather all the storms in your life. A Scripture verse that all Christians should know is Hebrews 11:1 which gives us the definition of faith – 'Now faith is the assurance of things hoped for, the conviction of things not seen'.

Jesus walking on water is one of the 37 miracles that he performed during the three years of his public ministry recorded in the Bible. By walking on water, he claimed to have supernatural power over the Laws of Nature. The disciples seeing this miracle exclaimed 'truly you are the Son of God'. Those who knew him closely believed that Jesus was a divine person and not merely only human. Jesus showed by this miracle that he had all authority in heaven and on earth (Matthew 28:18).

I'm fascinated by this beautiful image of Jesus walking on the water. He is saying to us through this picture that he is above any problem that we confront in earthly life and 'we will not sink beneath the waves' (Isaiah 43:2) if we have faith in him and trust in him.

Punch line: Faith can move mountains!

**Let us pray**: Dear Jesus, Son of the living God, have mercy on us poor sinners. Give us the gift of faith (Ephesians 2:8) to believe that we have been saved by our faith in you. Help us to focus on you so that all our problems will diminish in size and you will become bigger and bigger in our minds. Jesus, we trust in you. Jesus, we thank you. Jesus, we have faith in you. Amen.

---

CCC 227 It means trusting God in every circumstance, even in adversity. A prayer of St. Teresa of Jesus wonderfully expresses this trust:

Let nothing trouble you / Let nothing frighten you/ Everything passes / God never changes /Patience / Obtains all / Whoever has God / Wants for nothing / God alone is enough.

---

# God's Will Be Done

Today's message is about the difference between God and man.

In Hosea 11:9, God says, "I am God and not man," and in Isaiah 55:8-9, "For my thoughts are not your thoughts, neither are your ways my ways, declares the Lord. As the heavens are higher than the earth, so are my ways higher than your ways and my thoughts than your thoughts."

The problem with mankind is that we think we can run God's business better than him and we twist his arm and put him into a small box of our limited human way of thinking and plans.

This is the story of Naaman the leper who was healed of leprosy when he obeyed the Word of God after being angry with God because Naaman wanted Prophet Elisha to heal him in the way he thought was best. Naaman was the Commander of the army of the King of Aram and we read this story in the Book of Kings in the Bible. He goes to meet Elisha who was the miracle-working prophet of Israel.

2 Kings 5:9-14: *So Naaman went with his horses and chariots and stopped at the door of Elisha's house. Elisha sent a messenger to say to him, "Go, wash yourself seven times in the Jordan, and your flesh will be restored and you will be cleansed." But Naaman went away angry and said, "I thought that he would surely come out to me and stand and call on the*

*name of the Lord his God, wave his hand over the spot and cure me of my leprosy. Are not Abana and Pharpar, the rivers of Damascus, better than all the waters of Israel? Couldn't I wash in them and be cleansed?" So, he turned and went off in a rage.*

*Naaman's servants went to him and said, "My father, if the prophet had told you to do some great thing, would you not have done it? How much more, then, when he tells you, Wash and be cleansed!" So, he went down and dipped himself in the Jordan seven times, as the man of God had told him, and his flesh was restored and became clean like that of a young boy.*

My dear friends, 'moral relativism' is the philosophy of our age and its source, is this obsession with feelings. Moral relativism is not concerned with objective truth and error but how we feel. It is about personal preferences and disagreement with an absolute moral code. Moral relativism has developed into a subject in its own right. Evidence of moral relativism can be seen in our fear of suggesting to others that their feelings may be wrong (Note the case of Naaman's servants) or what is right or wrong is down to what each particular person thinks and not on an objective standard, like the Ten Commandments as a sure guide on how to live.

Our feelings tend to change with our hormones, our situation or our friends. The thinking of Naaman is so typical of our culture today. Thankfully, Naaman was able to look past his feelings and emotions and obey the command of God. Thus, this is the great lesson of the story of Naaman.

Here are three take-home points:

1) We can know God's thoughts if we seek him and are guided by the Holy Spirit (1 Corinthians 2:7).
2) Pray for the ability to know God's thoughts and how different they are from our thoughts (mostly influenced by how we feel).
3) Our thoughts should be mainly influenced by truth (Jesus said "I am the Way, the Truth and the Life" in John 14:6) and not mainly by our feelings and emotions.

Punch line: Wisdom trumps emotion!

**Let us pray**: Come Holy Spirit fall afresh on us, melt us, mould us, fill us and guide us to do the will of our Father. May the Holy Spirit of Truth guide us through our journey of life. Let us live by faith and belief in Jesus Christ and not merely by sight and feeling, for we walk by faith, not by sight (2 Corinthians 5:7). Help us to echo the prayer of Jesus in the Garden of Gethsemane, before he accepted his cross, when he said "Thy will be done." Amen.

CCC 2826 By prayer we can discern "what is the will of God" and obtain the endurance to do it. Jesus teaches us that one enters the kingdom of heaven not by speaking words, but by doing "the will of my Father in heaven."

# Our Triune God

Let me start by greeting you in the name of the Father and of the Son and of the Holy Spirit, as we believe in a Triune God.

In Deuteronomy 6:4, we read "Hear, O Israel: The LORD our God, the LORD is one." At the same time in the book of Genesis 1:26, we read "Let us make man in our image and likeness." Clearly, God is revealing himself as 'One' (the same image) and at the same time in the plural by saying 'let us' and 'our'.

In the book of Isaiah, God says, "for my thoughts are not your thoughts… for as the heavens are higher than the earth, so are my thoughts higher than your thoughts." Basically, the point God is making is that with our small brain (which weighs only three pounds), we cannot figure out fully to our understanding this mystery of God who has revealed Himself as Father, Son and Holy Spirit.

For me, the best comparison or analogy to understand this mystery is to think about water and the nature of water. The chemical nature of water is $H_2O$ (which means water has one oxygen atom and two hydrogen atoms). This chemical nature or substance can never change. But the beauty of water is that it can exist in three physical states—ice (when frozen), steam (when boiled) or water that we use every day.

It is important that although water is always the same substance $H_2O$, it can exist in three states because then it can perform three different functions.

Just like $H_2O$ that although 'One' has 'three' functions," Our God is 'One' in substance and nature (God is love) but he functions as 'three persons'. Our God who is love cannot exist as a solitary person. Our God is a perfect community of three persons – the Father, the Son and the Holy Spirit.

God the Father is the 'Creator' (Genesis 1:1) and is a hidden God (Isaiah 45:15) and has wrapped Himself in unapproachable Light (1 Timothy 6:16).

God the Son is Jesus Christ the tangible and visible likeness of God. He was sent by the Father as 'Saviour of the world' (John 3:16) and Jesus is our 'Redeemer' and sent to destroy the works of the Devil (1 John 3:8).

The Holy Spirit is the Love of God (Romans 5:5), the Power of God (2 Timothy 1:7), 'the Helper God' (John 14:26), who has made God known to man in whom we connect to God through Jesus who redeems us from sin. In other words, the Holy Spirit is God present on the earth and in our hearts. The Holy Spirit is the love between the Father and the Son and is the third person of the Holy Trinity.

Just like water, which has to function in three ways to achieve its purpose of being of use to man, God has to function as three persons in order to make himself personally known to man.

On the contrary, if he were just a God who sat on his throne in heaven, he would be a mere Deity and will remain unknown to man, without us having a personal encounter or a direct revelation of God. In my opinion, this personal encounter of God through Christ and the Holy Spirit is absolutely essential to be convinced that God exists.

The boast of Christianity is that God has fully revealed himself to man in the person of Jesus Christ who is God the Son as in Hebrews 1:3: "Jesus is the reflection of God's glory and the exact imprint of God's very being…".

The above image was inspired by St Patrick of Ireland. He demonstrated the three in one nature of God, using the illustration of the Shamrock leaf. Many things in creation show this threefold stamp of God. We live in a three-dimensional universe: time, space and matter.

Time has three aspects: the past, present and future. Space has length, breadth and height. The basic elements of an atom are neutron, proton and electron.

The basic needs of man are air, water and sunlight. The three basic components of a human being are body, mind and spirit (1 Thessalonians 5:23). The triune, Trinitarian or threefold seal of God has been imprinted in his creation of the universe.

Jesus told his disciples as he ascended to heaven, to baptise all people in the name of the Father, the Son and the Holy Spirit.

May the grace of our Lord Jesus Christ, the love of God and the fellowship of the Holy Spirit be with you. Amen.

Punch line: The Perfect Triune God of Love!

**Let us pray**: We thank you Father who are in Heaven for hearing us and we worship you as the Holy Trinity—three persons in one God. Pour out your love into our hearts and make your home in our hearts. As your disciples, help us to show to others this love that comes from you. Almighty God, protect us and our families from the dangers, sudden misfortunes and diseases as we place our trust in you. Amen.

---

CCC 234 The mystery of the Most Holy Trinity is the central mystery of Christian faith and life. It is the mystery of God in himself. It is therefore the source of all the other mysteries of faith, the light that enlightens them. It is the most fundamental and essential teaching in the "hierarchy of the truths of faith". The whole history of salvation is identical with the history of the way and the means by which the one true God, Father, Son and Holy Spirit, reveals himself to men "and reconciles and unites with himself those who turn away from sin".

---

# Baptism in the Holy Spirit

There are two sets of readings for this reflection: the feast of the Ascension and the Sunday reading.

The Ascension, is a major event in the life of Jesus because it describes the glory in which Jesus was taken up in the clouds and went back to heaven to the right hand of the Father. The disciples worshipped Jesus as God when they saw 'His Glory'. In the Bible, 'Glory' is given only to God and to describe the greatness of the Kingdom of God.

There are two verses that catch our attention:

1) Acts 1:8: "You will receive power when the Holy Spirit comes on you."
2) John 17:3: "And eternal life is this: to know you, the only true God and Jesus Christ whom you sent."

My personal experience of Jesus happened after hearing the Word of God for five days at a retreat (spending time in prayer); and when holy men laid hands on me, I received an outpouring of the Holy Spirit some years ago. This gave me a foretaste of Heaven and through the Holy Spirit, I have come to know Jesus personally. At the time of laying on of hands on my head, calling upon the Holy Spirit to fill me, I received the gift of praying in tongues. This is a divine gift because it cannot be conjured by human will or intellect!

Jesus says that 'to know him' means the same as having eternal life. There are two ways in which we use the word 'know': you can 'know about someone' or you can 'know someone'.

*A Christian author and speaker Nicki Gumbel writes about his wife Pippa, whom he has been married to for many years. He says, just imagine that he read a book written 'about his wife' (titled Pippa: The Amazing Woman!) before their marriage. He would have been thrilled to read the chapters in the book that described how beautiful she was, that Pippa was a great cook, she is an excellent housewife, and another chapter that said how intelligent she was and other descriptions about her many talents and interests! But, by reading this book, he only knows about her as being a wonderful person.*

*Then Nicki Gumbel goes on to say that now that they have been married and been together for very many years, 'he knows' from first-hand experience, Pippa is far more precious and wonderful than what he had read about her in the book! The close relationship of a marriage is the most intimate human relationship known in this world. It is only through an intimate relationship that we come to know a person fully.*

Similarly, in the Gospel reading (John 17:3), Jesus says "knowing me is eternal life."

Another way to explain is the taste of sugar. The sweetness of sugar can be best appreciated only when we taste sugar. Only reading all details about sugar can give you a lot of information about it, like how it is made and what is its chemical structure. But, if you have never tasted sugar, you will never know how sweet sugar tastes!

That is why in Psalm 34:8 we read "taste and see that the Lord is good."

As we are preparing for the great feast of Pentecost Sunday, let us spend more time every day in prayer. In today's readings, we hear that the disciples along with Mother Mary were devoting themselves to continuous prayer. It was as they waited and prayed that the Holy Spirit came down on them with great power as 'tongues of fire' and gave them the courage to preach the Good News that Jesus Christ is the Saviour of all mankind (not just of only the Christians but people of other faiths or no particular faith). St Peter says in Acts 10:34, "I truly understand that God shows no partiality, but in every nation anyone who fears him and does what is right is acceptable to him".

Jesus Christ died for the forgiveness of the sins of the whole world! This includes people of all religions and beliefs (including atheists and agnostics), and the Bible says in Revelation 3:20, "he stands at the door and knocks," and if you invite him to your heart, "he will dine with you." Yes, the invitation of Jesus: "come dine with me," is open to all, every day and at any time! The free phone number to call on the Lord is 333 (Jeremiah 33:3, "Call on me and I will answer you")!

Punch line: Let the fire of Pentecost fall!

**Let us pray**: Lord Jesus, I ask you to give us the grace to call on you, to spend more time in prayer and help us to thirst for you. Please send the Holy Spirit to fill our hearts. Lord, cleanse my heart from all the evil desires, and I pray that you give us a close encounter with you so that we can say, I have tasted the Lord and I know he is good.

Maranatha! Come Lord Jesus and be the Lord of my life. Jesus, I trust in you. Amen.

---

CCC 731 On the day of Pentecost when the seven weeks of Easter had come to an end, Christ's Passover is fulfilled in the outpouring of the Holy Spirit, manifested, given, and communicated as a divine person: of his fullness, Christ, the Lord, pours out the Spirit in abundance.

---

# Peter and Paul in Rome

St Peter and St Paul are the most well-known of all the apostles of Jesus Christ and both were used by the Holy Spirit to spread the Good News of salvation. Christianity spread rapidly from Israel, to other parts of the Middle East and Europe through the ministry of Peter and Paul.

Unfortunately, as they preached Jesus as the Messiah and the Son of the living God, they came up against extreme persecution from the Jews and the Romans.

St Peter was thrown into prison, soon after St James was beheaded by King Herod and St Stephen was stoned to death. This was the punishment for being a Christian, especially in the first century! In Acts chapter 12, we read about the miraculous way in which God sent an angel to release Peter from prison and this happened because the people of God were praying for Peter. This experience of being put in prison did not prevent Peter from continuing to proclaim Christ as the Messiah and Saviour of the world.

St Peter is proclaimed as 'the first Pope' by the Universal Mother Church, built on Peter, by Christ Himself – The Catholic Church! Peter is the first one to whom the Father from heaven revealed the true identity of Jesus as being the 'Son of the living God' (Matthew 16:18). He was persecuted all through his ministry and was finally given the death sentence by the Romans, and crucified just like Jesus.

However, Peter said that he was not worthy to be crucified like Christ and requested to be crucified upside down!

St Paul had a similar experience to Peter as he too was thrown into prison! Again, we read in Acts 16 that being in prison did not prevent Paul from praying or praising God. Paul was singing songs of praise and thanksgiving in his prison and again the Lord sent an angel to release Paul from prison in a miraculous way. St Paul was known as 'Saul' before his conversion to Christ and he was at that time joining the Jews in persecuting Christians. In fact, Saul had ordered the murder of many Christians and approved of the stoning of St Stephen to death!

Jesus in his mercy appeared to Saul and called him to preach the Gospel. After he was chosen by Jesus through a personal encounter (Acts 9, the Conversion of Saul), his name was changed from 'Saul to Paul'. Just like St Peter, he too endured extreme hardships and persecution, in proclaiming Christ to the world. Paul travelled much in his missionary journeys and eventually was executed like Peter. St Paul was beheaded by the Romans and died in Rome.

All the twelve apostles except St John were killed for proclaiming Christ! It is said that 'the blood shed by the early Christian martyrs is the seed of the Catholic Church built on the solid foundation of Jesus Christ'. That is why we read in today's gospel that Jesus told the disciples that 'the gates of hell will not prevail against the church built on Peter the rock' (Matthew 16:19). Here again, Jesus changed the name of Peter from Simon to Peter, which in Greek means 'rock'. A Scripture all should know is 1 Timothy 3:15 "the pillar and foundation of the truth is the church of the living God."

The question before each of us today is: 'Who do you say Jesus is?' If you accept him as the Way, the Truth and the Life and as the Saviour of the world, 'he will be with you always till the end' (Matthew 28:19), and he will give you the faith and the strength to go through all types of difficult situations all through your life! Jesus, who is the Truth, is present in a special way in the church he founded on the glorious apostles, 'St Peter and St Paul – the Holy Catholic Church'. Halleluia!

Punch line: The Church of Rome – The Pillar and Foundation of the Truth!

**Let us pray:** Lord Jesus, we thank you for giving us two great saints in Peter and Paul. Fill us with the Holy Spirit and increase our faith in you. Just as you were close to St Peter and St Paul, in the most trying times in their lives, be with us too. Strengthen us and send us angels in the form of kind people to support us during the times of dire need.

May the Holy Spirit enlighten our minds, to understand that the Truth, who is Christ, is preserved by the Church founded on St Peter. Amen.

> CCC 642 Everything that happened during those Paschal days involves each of the apostles – and Peter in particular – in the building of the new era begun on Easter morning. As witnesses of the Risen One, they remain the foundation stones of his Church. The faith of the first community of believers is based on the witness of concrete men known to the Christians and for the most part still living among them. Peter and the Twelve are the primary "witnesses to his Resurrection", but they are not the only ones – Paul speaks clearly of more than five hundred persons to whom Jesus appeared on a single occasion and also of James and of all the apostles.

# A Call to Repentance

Repentance is the activity of reviewing one's actions and feeling contrition or regret for past wrongs, which is accompanied by commitment to carry out actions that show and prove, we have made a change for the better.

The first is responsibility: We must recognise that we have done wrong. The second is regret: We must have true remorse for doing wrong and for the pain and problems we've caused. The third is resolve: We must be committed never to repeating the act or acts regardless of the temptations or situation.

Tell God that you want to turn away from your old life and follow Him. Tell Him you want a new life and to become a new creation in Him. Tell Him you are willing to do whatever it takes to get right with Him—make a U-turn to God.

True repentance is being sincere about getting free from sin and not justifying or arguing their case any longer. It means that a person is genuine and sincere about being more Christ-like. They want to clear themselves. This isn't paying for their own sin; they don't want to hide their sin but have it removed at all costs. The Sacrament of Confession is a very important way of receiving the Lord's mercy and forgiveness and be given the strength of grace not to sin again.

David Wilkerson, wrote a very popular book entitled, *The Cross and the Switchblade*—the work of a Christian

Evangelist in the streets of New York. Below is this true story of the repentance and conversion of Nicky Cruz.

*Nicky Cruz (born December 6, 1938) is a Christian evangelist, the founder of Nicky Cruz Outreach, an evangelistic Christian ministry. He was also once the director of Teen Challenge, serving under David Wilkerson, before founding another ministry home himself, in California. Prior to his conversion, he was the leader of a New York City gang, the Mau Maus.*

*Cruz was born in Las Piedras, Puerto Rico, where he was raised by his parents. His parents practiced 'Brujeria' and were followers of spiritism ('espiritismo'). They mentally abused him; his own mother would call him 'Son of Satan'. The neighbourhood in which he lived was one of the worst in Puerto Rico, and Cruz was always getting into trouble.*

*According to his book Run Baby Run, his parents sent him to live with his brother in New York City when he was 15, and Cruz soon ran away and started living on the streets of the city. He became a member of the Mau Maus street gang, and about six months later, Cruz was selected 'Warlord of the gang'. He quickly rose to become their president.*

*Shortly after Cruz became the gang leader, David Wilkerson was preaching in the neighbourhood when Cruz encountered him. The preacher told Cruz that 'Jesus loved him and would never stop loving him'. Cruz responded by slapping Wilkerson and threatening to kill him. Wilkerson attempted again later to convert Cruz and received the same response.*

*Later, Wilkerson organised an evangelistic meeting in the neighbourhood, with the intent of converting the Mau Maus.*

*When Cruz heard about it, he headed with some of the members of his gang for the boxing arena where the meeting was being held, on a bus sent specially by Wilkerson.*

*According to Cruz, when he arrived at the arena, "he felt guilty about the things that he had done and began to pray." After preaching, Wilkerson asked the Mau Maus to take up a collection. Cruz volunteered and led a group of the gang through the crowd, insisting on people giving money. Going backstage, he saw an exit but convinced the group to give the money to Wilkerson on stage. Later, Wilkerson gave an altar call, and a large number of gang members responded. Wilkerson prayed with Cruz, and Cruz asked God to forgive him.*

*Afterwards, Cruz and some of the gang members who were converted went to the police and turned in all of their bricks, handguns and knives, shocking the police officers in the station. They stated that if they had seen the group approaching, they probably would have shot them down. Cruz began to study the Bible and went to Bible College. He became a preacher and returned to his old neighbourhood, where he preached and converted more of the Mau Maus to Christianity, including the gang's new leader, Israel Narvaez.*

Gang leader turned evangelist Nicky Cruz at an evangelistic crusade in Honduras during the 1970s.

Punch line: The Cross is mightier than the switchblade!

**Let us pray**: Lord Jesus, we thank you for sending your Holy Spirit to convince Nicky Cruz of his sin leading him to true repentance. Send upon us the same Holy Spirit to help us turn away from anger, violence, drugs, immorality and other evils, to God. May the Holy Spirit, our Helper and Guide, come upon us to experience the love of God in Christ Jesus and make us a new person (2 Corinthians 5:17) to walk in the light of the Lord. Amen.

CCC 1431 Interior repentance is a radical reorientation of our whole life, a return, a conversion to God with all our heart, an end of sin, a turning away from evil, with repugnance toward the evil actions we have committed. At the same time, it entails the desire and resolution to change one's life, with hope in God's mercy and trust in the help of his grace. This conversion of heart is accompanied by a salutary pain and sadness which the Fathers called animi cruciatus (affliction of spirit) and compunctio cordis (repentance of heart).

# Our Spiritual Nourishment

The Bible readings today refer to the 'Word of God', being compared to the sowing of seeds by a Sower that has to take root and grow into a plant. Also, we heard from the reading that, 'like the snow and the rain that water the ground, the Word of God does not return empty, without achieving its purpose of blessing the soul that is ready and open to receive' (Isaiah 55:8).

If a soul (mind) is well prepared and open and ready to receive the Word, the Scripture will undoubtedly have a positive impact and bring about a change in the attitude of the person.

The question to ask ourselves today is: 'Are we well prepared, open and ready for the message from God, to bring about in us an observable change in our thoughts, words and actions?'

The key word is 'understanding' and true understanding comes from the Lord (1 John 5:20). In order to understand anything clearly the state of our mind is important. I recall a time of great stress and worry in my life in the recent past. When my little grandson was in a coma on a ventilator, I was attending a training course. It was absolutely impossible for me to be attentive and concentrate on the teaching.

The seed is God's Word and the soil in which it is sown is our mind. It is important to have a clear mind to understand the meaning of the Word. When the understanding is inspired by the Holy Spirit, our faith that takes root in our mind grows into a spiritual plant, and we grow in our spiritual life.

Jesus said, if the Word does not take root, then it is like sowing the seed on a rock and we soon fall away when a trial or persecution comes our way. If you are a worrier or preoccupied with achievement and riches of this world, Jesus said it is like sowing the seeds among thorns, and the Word cannot take root.

Therefore, my dear friends, we have to prepare our minds to receive the Word. One way of doing this, is to avoid temptation by taking care of what we see, hear, touch, taste and smell—the five senses that lead to sin which pollute our mind! This pollution of the mind caused by sin often manifests in our behaviour when we feel shame and guilt, often unconscious, which in turn, can be manifested as anxiety or anger.

The two major functions of the human mind are thinking and feeling—our thoughts and our emotions. St Paul says that we must 'take captive every thought and make it obedient to Christ' (2 Corinthians 10:5). The most difficult emotion to control is anger. The Bible teaches, "be angry but do not let the sun go down on your anger and do not make room for the devil" as said in Ephesians 4:26-27. The Bible exhorts us to overcome sin in Genesis 4:7, "sin is lurking at the door; its desire is for you, but you must overcome it."

The blood of Jesus shed on Calvary cleanses us from all sin (1 John 1:7) and gives us a clear mind for the Holy Spirit to live and work in our lives. In Isaiah 1:18, the Lord says, 'although your stains are crimson, you will be as white as snow'. In prayer, always remember to ask the Lord to have mercy on us and forgive our sins.

The process of the growth of a seed into a plant is called Germination. Germination can take place successfully only if the seed is provided with the right conditions for its growth. It requires carbon-dioxide, water, sunlight and the right temperature for growth. Similarly, for the spiritual growth of 'the seed of the Word of God' sown in a clear mind, it is important that we have the right conditions, namely; a life of prayer, Christian fellowship and charitable giving!

## Parable of the Sower Faith Types

| Faith Blinders | Faith Rocky | Faith Rebel | Remaining Faith |
|---|---|---|---|
| Value of God's Message not understood, and is disregarded. | Contentment in surface faith in God, skips dedication to depth needed to stand firm. | Destructively allows worldly priorities to compete with faith in God as primary. | Enduring faith in Jesus, fruitfully understands and practices God's Word. |

http://BibleOpia.WordPress.com          11/30/2011

Good soil = mind unpolluted by sin
Conditions for spiritual growth = Prayer + Fellowship + charitable works

Punch line: God is the author of life and growth!

**Let us pray:** Lord Jesus, we come into your presence asking you to wash us clean of all our sins and iniquities and make us white as snow, so that we can have confidence in your presence. Lord, please heal our shame and guilt and free us from the spirit of anxiety and anger, which have caused many problems in our lives. Lord, we ask that you clear our mind of all worries and preoccupation with the cares of this world and give us the grace to focus on the glorious majesty of how great you are, Our Lord and Our God, so that the seed of faith will bud and blossom into a healthy tree of life. Lord, help us to pray, to remain in Christian fellowship and do charitable works. Mother Mary, please intercede for us and protect us from evil. Amen.

CCC 2624 In the first community of Jerusalem, believers "devoted themselves to the apostles' teaching and fellowship, to the breaking of bread, and the prayers." This sequence is characteristic of the Church's prayer: founded on the apostolic faith; authenticated by charity; nourished in the Eucharist.

# The Star of Wonder

You've heard the well-known carol—Star of Wonder.

Let's read about this 'Star of Bethlehem' from Matthew's Gospel 2:1-12.

The focus will be on:

1) The gifts presented to the Son of Mary.
2) The meaning of star.
3) Jesus: the true light.

This is the famous story of the three kings or the three Wise Men from the East, who came to pay homage or worship and adoration to the baby Jesus. This act of 'worship and homage' signified that the child Jesus was in fact, God and King; because worship is due only to a God and bowing is the honour and respect given to a King. In this event, known as 'the Epiphany', the wise men were proclaiming to the whole world, the Divinity of the child Jesus, born in a manger! They were led by an extraordinarily bright star, which stood over the manger where Jesus was born. The star pointed the way to Jesus.

It is clear from the Gospel account that there was a celestial event, described as the Star of Bethlehem, which caught the attention of the wise men who travelled a long distance to bring their gifts of Gold, Frankincense and Myrrh.

'Gold' is the gift that is fittingly given to a King and by this gesture, they expressed their conviction that Jesus is a King.

'Frankincense' is a sign of praise and worship that is offered by a Jewish High Priest once a year in the temple when he enters into the presence of God in the Holiest part of the Temple. By this action, the Wise Men were acknowledging that 'God was born as a human being' and the word used for this is 'Incarnation'. Christmas for Christians is also known as 'The Incarnation'. Jesus is called 'Emmanuel' which means 'God with us.'

'Myrrh' is the substance that is used to preserve a dead body and it represents mortality. By this action, they were prophesying that this King, this God incarnate, 'came to die' so that we may be saved and go to heaven. Such is the love of God to bring salvation to mankind in the birth of Christ. In John 3:16 we read "for God so loved the world that he gave his only Son, so that everyone who believes in Him may not perish but may have eternal life", which is the Golden verse of the Bible.

'The Gold' that we can give Him as a gift is our good works to help people in pain and suffering. 'The Frankincense' that we can offer Him is our song of thanksgiving and praise, who breathed his very life into the human soul. 'The Myrrh' that we can present Him is our sacrifices, difficulties and the day-to-day pain of life, so that the people we deal with, may get healing, recovery and a better quality of life.

A star is a massive luminous sphere of plasma held together by its own gravity. A star shines due to the thermonuclear fusion of hydrogen into helium at its core, releasing energy that radiates outwards. St Paul says that we are called to shine like stars in this world. This can be done by holding ourselves together with help of the Spirit of God and by converting the evil in our hearts into good by making a good confession; then we will be able to shine as a light in this world. 'A star' is someone who puts on an especially good performance or a brilliant piece of work; like an A* grade in examinations. We should shine in front of others not just for our achievements but for our good works done out of love for other people.

Christmas falls on the shortest and darkest day in the year; yes, Christ came as a light into a dark world. Jesus himself said in John 8:12, "I am the Light of the world and anyone who comes to me will not walk in darkness." "The Word of God is a lamp to my feet and a light to my path" (Psalm 119:109). He told his disciples, "You are the light of this world". Only light can put out darkness; just as sadness can be put out by joy and hatred conquered with love.

We can become stars that shine in a dark world by bringing to the Lord this Christmas, our small and humble virtuous actions, as gifts of Gold, Frankincense and Myrrh. We are called to be stars that light the way for people and point them in a God-direction, like the Star of Bethlehem that stood over the baby Jesus.

Punch line: Shine, Jesus, Shine!

**Let us pray**: Lord Jesus, our God in the manger, give us the grace to do ordinary things with extraordinary love like innocent children, so that we will shine like stars in this dark world (Philippians 2:15). Amen.

---

CCC 528 The Epiphany is the manifestation of Jesus as Messiah of Israel, Son of God and Saviour of the world. The great feast of Epiphany celebrates the adoration of Jesus by the wise men (magi) from the East, together with his baptism in the Jordan and the wedding feast at Cana in Galilee. In the magi, representatives of the neighbouring pagan religions, the Gospel sees the first-fruits of the nations, who welcome the good news of salvation through the Incarnation.

# The Generosity of God

I googled 'free stuff' and found many advertisements enticing people to fill out a form or do something easy to do, with an offer of free stuff. Below is an example:

'Southern Comfort is giving away 1,000 FREE cocktail kits! For a chance to win, simply enter your date of birth then complete their short entry.'

I found that there is always an unknown selfish or ulterior motive whenever something 'free' is advertised in this world, and we may end up giving out personal information like date of birth! But not so with our God who is described as being full of compassion and love. In today's reading, the Lord is calling us to come to him. The salvation that he offers us is truly free.

We see today that 'Jesus never forsakes or turns away anyone' (Hebrews 13:5) who comes to him for help or healing. Our God's nature is to give, from the riches of his glory (Philippians 4:19). Jesus taught us that it is better to give than to receive.

Since we are the children of God, our Eternal Father, he expects us to share his nature of generosity—the art of giving of our time, money, food and helping hand in serving others. Here are some scriptures to teach you the importance of generosity and the amazing blessing that comes to a generous person:

2 Corinthians 9:7: "Each of you must give as you have made up your mind, not reluctantly or under compulsion, for God loves a cheerful giver."

Malachi 3:10: "Bring the whole tithe into the storehouse that there may be food in my house. Test me in this," says the Lord Almighty, "and see if I will not throw open the floodgates of heaven and pour out so much blessing that there will not be room enough to store it."

Luke 6:38: "Give, and it will be given to you. A good measure, pressed down, shaken together, running over, will be put into your lap; for the measure you give will be the measure you get back."

Acts 20:35: "In all this I have given you an example that by such work we must support the weak, remembering the words of the Lord Jesus, for he himself said, it is more blessed to give than to receive."

God loves a cheerful giver. (2 Cor. 9:7)

The above picture is the true story of the Widow's Offering, in Luke 21:2-4 – Jesus saw a poor widow put in two small copper coins and he said "Truly I tell you; this poor widow has put in more than all of them; for all of them have contributed out of their abundance, but she out of her poverty put in all she had to live on." The Holy Spirit makes good fruit to grow in our lives and one of the fruits of the Holy Spirit is generosity (Galatians 5:22).

My personal experience is that God appreciates us most when we give to those who are poor and needy; who will not be able to repay our generosity. I helped one of my close relatives in India for many years. He had nobody for support and was literally homeless and in need of safe housing. I provided him with a roof above his head, food and medicine for a few years until he was able to move to a better place.

This was the turning point in my life. I had a breakthrough in my life when floodgates of heaven were opened for me and I was paid in good measure, pressed down, running over and put into my lap. The doors opened for me to come to the UK, and this blessing to work and live in the UK, is one of the things I cherish in my life and thank God for this blessing.

The spirit of generosity in me became more important after I realised and understood 'the truth that Jesus Christ is God's free gift to us' (Romans 6:23). Accepting Jesus wholeheartedly as my Saviour and Lord changed the complexion of my life.

As we read today, the love of God can be made visible only in Christ Jesus our Lord, who shed his blood for all humanity, so that we may all have 'salvation as a free gift'. The generous spirit of Jesus is so powerful and overwhelming, that the five loaves and two fish that he blessed, was multiplied manifold to feed more than 5,000 people and there was a surplus or leftover food. This miracle is a foreshadowing of the Holy Eucharist!

In the Holy Eucharist, Jesus gives himself to us in this 'Holy Bread' and he is able to satisfy all our inmost needs, especially to restore our relationship with God the Father.

Punch line: A Cheerful Giver – token of God's love!

**Let us pray**: Father, we thank you that through the 'free gift of Jesus', we have become your children. Send your Holy Spirit upon us and may the power of the Spirit give us the fruit of generosity, especially to give and help the poor, the weak and the needy. We believe that you will open the windows of heaven to bless us when we give cheerfully. Help us always to remember that it is 'better to give than to receive'. Amen.

---

CCC 2446 St. John Chrysostom vigorously recalls this: "Not to enable the poor to share in our goods is to steal from them and deprive them of life. The goods we possess are not ours, but theirs." "The demands of justice must be satisfied first of all; that which is already due in justice is not to be offered as a gift of charity":

When we attend to the needs of those in want, we give them what is theirs, not ours. More than performing works of mercy, we are paying a debt of justice.

---

# The Kingdom of God

The main subject of today's Gospel reading is the Kingdom of God.

Once again Jesus refers to the 'Kingdom of God' as a 'good seed' that is sown in the field. As we understood from previous reflection, the 'good seed' has to be cared for every day with prayer, and then even if that seed of faith is only the size of a mustard seed, it can grow into the biggest shrub of all! How important it is to 'nurture our seed of faith with daily prayer'!

The third comparison of the Kingdom of God is to 'yeast', which requires only a small quantity to be mixed with flour to make the dough rise. Yeast is a very strong substance and can influence all of the dough to rise. Here the point is that with strong faith, a Christian is like 'yeast' and is able to positively influence, all those around, through the presence of Christ in our hearts, spreading out as a fragrance—the aroma of Christ.

Another theme that we understand from the reading is that both good and evil exist together. C.S. Lewis, one of the most well-known Christian writers of the twentieth century said, "We live in enemy-occupied territory!" This means that there is the reality of the Kingdom of darkness or the Kingdom of Satan.

Today, Jesus is challenging us to do away with the works of darkness and become people of the light. Jesus referred to

Satan as 'the prince of this world' (John 12:31) and St Paul referred to Satan as 'the god of this world' (2 Corinthians 4:4).

It is a very valid question to ask ourselves, which Kingdom do we belong to? Is it the Kingdom of God or the Kingdom of Satan? Repentance is about stepping out of darkness into light and staying in the light. It is not easy but the Holy Spirit, which has been poured into our hearts will help us remain firm and steadfast in our faith. We are especially weak in the face of problems and adversity. However, in Romans 8:26 we read 'the Spirit comes to help us in our weakness'.

Even if we falter or fall back, it is important to keep coming back because the door of the Kingdom of God, is the arms of our loving Father God and this door is always open. For Catholics, the sacrament of confession is the best way of returning when we lose our way. Psalm 51 is a powerful prayer of repentance. In personal prayer, always ask for forgiveness, especially if we have committed any grave sin. Then, when we go to the Sacrament of Confession, the priest offers forgiveness in these words: "Through the Ministry of the Church may the Lord in his goodness bring you pardon and peace. I absolve you from your sins in the name of Father and of the Son and of the Holy Spirit."

My dear friends, there are two important scriptures in the Bible that categorises the type of things we do, or the type of people, who will not enter the Kingdom of God. Another scripture, tells us the qualities of a person in the Kingdom of God.

The Scriptures are Galatians 5:19-21: "Now the works of the flesh are obvious: fornication, impurity, licentiousness, idolatry, sorcery, enmities, strife, jealousy, anger, quarrels, dissensions, factions, envy, drunkenness, carousing and things like these. I am warning you, as I warned you before: those who do such things will not inherit the kingdom".

Galatians 5:22-24: By contrast, the fruit of the Spirit is "love, joy, peace, patience, kindness, generosity, faithfulness, gentleness, and self-control. There is no law against such things. And those who belong to Christ Jesus have crucified the flesh with its passions and desires".

| Kingdom of God | Kingdom of Satan |
|---|---|
| Producing good fruit | Producing bad fruit |
| Love | Fornication, Impurity |
| Joy | Licentiousness, Idolatry |
| Peace | Sorcery, Enmities |
| Patience | Anger, Quarrels |
| Kindness | Dissensions, Factions |
| Generosity | Envy, Drunkenness |
| Faithfulness | Carousing |
| Gentleness | |
| Self-control | |

There are numerous testimonies of sinners who made a decision to step out of darkness into light. St Augustine who is a doctor of the Church and was a Bishop in the Catholic Church was one of the big sinners who became a saint. He was an idolater, was involved in all sorts of strange practices and in sexual immorality and a liar. His mother was St Monica, a very prayerful woman, who daily prayed for her son's conversion.

She prayed this short simple prayer to the Lord: 'May your Kingdom come into the life of my son'. She prayed this prayer with tears for seventeen years! It is said that St Monica wet the carpet with her tears each time she prayed for Augustine. She was given a vision by the Lord of the 'the Light of Christ shining on the radiant face of her son'. This encouraged her to pray without giving up. Her prayers were eventually answered and Augustine gave his life to Christ and moved from Kingdom of Darkness to the Kingdom of Light.

Punch line: Enter the Kingdom of God!

**Let us pray**: Lord Jesus, we acknowledge you as our Saviour and thank you wholeheartedly for dying for us on the cross and shedding your blood for us. Continue to wash us daily in your precious blood and fill us with the Holy Spirit so that we may always walk in the Light of the Lord. Help us to decide to step into and remain in the Kingdom of God. We pray that you protect us and our families from the evil one. Help us to persevere in prayer for the Kingdom of God to come into our lives. Amen.

---

CCC 391 Behind the disobedient choice of our first parents lurks a seductive voice, opposed to God, which makes them fall into death out of envy. Scripture and the Church's Tradition see in this being a fallen angel, called "Satan" or the "devil". The Church teaches that Satan was at first a good angel, made by God: "The devil and the other demons were indeed created naturally good by God, but they became evil by their own doing."

# Jesus – Name above all Names

In this reflection, I would like to write to you about the power of the name of Jesus.

We know from Matthew 1:21-23 that Jesus is the 'Son of God' and he is called Emmanuel that means 'God is with us.' The heart of Christian prayer is praying 'to the Father through the Son (Jesus) in the Holy Spirit' (Ephesians 2:18). Our prayer is like incense reaching the Father, only through the Son. Jesus said, "I am the Way, the Truth, and the Life. No one comes to the Father except through me" (John 14:6).

Pope Francis reminds us that "at the start of Mass we ask the Lord to be merciful to us because our sins, while separating us from God, also divides us from our brothers and sisters … severs the relationship within the family, in society and in the community." (General Audience, 3 January, 2018). The only sacrifice that has the power to wash us from sin is the blood of Jesus and the name of Jesus. In Jesus Christ, there is no condemnation (Romans 8:1), and the Bible says all those having guilt and shame from our sinfulness have been 'washed, sanctified and justified in the name of Jesus' (1 Corinthians 6:11).

Christians claim to have power in the name of Jesus. Below are three important Scriptures to show you the power of His Name.

Acts 4:12: "There is salvation in no one else, for there is no other name under heaven given among mortals by which we must be saved."

Acts 3:6-8: "But Peter said, I have no silver or gold, but what I have I give you; in the name of Jesus Christ of Nazareth, stand up and walk. And he took him by the right hand and raised him up, and immediately his feet and ankles were made strong."

" Such as I have give I thee."—*Acts* iii. 6.

Acts 14:13-14: "I will do whatever you ask in my name, so that the Father may be glorified in the Son. If in my name you ask me for anything, I will do it."

Here is a true story that happened during the American Civil War to show you how powerful a son can be to influence his father in our world and in human terms:

*As a result of a family tragedy, 'a soldier' had been given permission to have a 'hearing with the president' because he wanted to request an exemption from military service. But when he arrived at the White House, he was refused entry, and he was sent away, and he went to sit in a nearby park. And, as he was sitting in this park, a young boy came across him and just remarked about how unhappy he looked. And the soldier found himself pouring out his heart to this young guy.*

*And, eventually, the boy said, 'Look, come with me,' and the dejected soldier went back to the White House; they went round the back. None of the guards seemed to stop them — even the generals and the high-ranking government officials stood to attention and let them pass through —and the soldier was amazed.*

*Finally, they came to the presidential office. Without knocking they went into the west wing, the young boy opened the door of the Oval Office, walked straight in, and there was Abraham Lincoln (the president of USA), standing there in conversation with the Secretary of State. And the moment they walked in, Abraham Lincoln turned to the boy and said, 'Todd, what can I do for you?' And Todd said, 'Dad, this soldier needs to talk to you.' The soldier had access to the president of United States of America, through the president's son.*

How much more powerful is the Son of God, Jesus, who is the exact likeness of the Father (Colossians 1:15), to make sure that our prayers reach Our Heavenly Father!

In the past 2000 years the most powerful name that has been and is being uttered by human lips is the name of Jesus! Using the Name of "Jesus" repeatedly or in short prayers such as 'Jesus, I love you'; 'Jesus, I trust in you', 'Jesus have mercy

117

on me,' can bring peace to our soul in times of frustration, despair, loneliness, depression, fear; when our mind is pervaded by negative thoughts and emotions. It is like spraying de-icer on a frosted windscreen; the Jesus prayer can clear your mind.

Punch line: Jesus, what a beautiful name!

**Let us pray**: Father, we come to you through Christ, in the Spirit, that we may live our lives rooted and grounded in Our Lord Jesus Christ (Colossians 2:7) and faith in his name, in whom the fathomless mercy of God has been revealed. Amen.

---

CCC 432 The name "Jesus" signifies that the very name of God is present in the person of his Son, made man for the universal and definitive redemption from sins. It is the divine name that alone brings salvation, and henceforth all can invoke his name, for Jesus united himself to all men through his Incarnation, so that "there is no other name under heaven given among men by which we must be saved."

# Jesus Sends the Holy Spirit

On Pentecost Sunday, we celebrate 'the birthday of the Church' and this is the day on which the Holy Spirit came upon the disciples of Jesus with mighty, enormous, power. We read today that 'they were all filled with the Holy Spirit' on the feast day of Pentecost (Acts 2). This was the most powerful encounter for man with the Holy Spirit in the entire history of the Church.

The Holy Spirit has been there from the beginning of time when God created the world (Genesis 1:2 "the Spirit of God hovered over the waters"). The Bible says that the Spirit of God will be there at the end of time (Revelation 22:17 "let anyone who is thirsty come and drink from the water of life"). This means that the Spirit of God has been here on our earth throughout our salvation history both in the Old and New Testament.

Before the Pentecost, the Holy Spirit was sent by God only on particular people at particular times and not given to everyone. After the Pentecost, the Old Testament prophesy of Joel became true (Joel 2:28 "the Lord will pour out his Spirit on all flesh") and so now all of us have the potential to be filled with the Spirit.

A fundamental condition, 'to be filled with the Spirit of God', is that we must have 'an intense thirst or hunger for the Spirit of God'. The Bible exhorts (Ephesians 5:18) us to be drunk with Spirit and to substitute 'Holy Spirit intoxication' for other forms of intoxication like alcohol!

As soon as they were filled with the Spirit, the disciples were talking loudly, without inhibition praising God. This event, was accompanied by the great miracle of the disciples receiving the gift of tongues. The people from different nations, 'could hear them in their own native language' and it made sense. However, unlike the effect of alcohol, which can make a person speak nonsense, the Holy Spirit made them speak sense with courage, wisdom and love. When St Peter spoke his first sermon, after being filled with the Holy Spirit, soon after the Pentecost, three thousand people gave their lives to Christ and asked to be baptised!

In Acts 2:13, we read that some people "made fun of them saying they had too much wine." St Paul expected the "Christians to be drunk with the Holy Spirit" and that is why St Paul said in Ephesians 5:18, "do not be drunk with wine, which leads to debauchery (antisocial behaviour) but instead be filled with the Spirit." In John 7:37, Jesus said, "If anyone is thirsty let him come to me and drink." Again, like an alcoholic who craves or is thirsty for alcohol, the Bible encourages us to crave or to thirst for the Holy Spirit. The promise of the Holy Spirit (Acts 2:39) is for anyone who repents and believes that Jesus came from heaven as the Saviour of this world.

Therefore, the Holy Spirit can be addictive and once anyone is filled with the Holy Spirit, the experience can be very powerful and joyful. The temporary happiness given by alcohol cannot compare with the permanent joy of the Spirit of God. The Holy Spirit has the power to set us free, by breaking every chain of any kind of addiction.

When I received an outpouring of the Holy Spirit, it was an intense enormously exhilarating experience; a foretaste of Heaven! This happened during the 5-day retreat (January 1993), at the time of anointing prayer ministry. I felt an electric current flow through my entire body pulling me up on my toes with uplifted hands in prayer. The Holy Spirit enabled me to pray in tongues for a good fifteen minutes accompanied by an audible angelic choir! My life has never been the same after I received the Baptism in the Holy Spirit – I was given the strength to remain anchored in my faith and belief. Halleluia!

There are many testimonies of people being 'set free from addictions' by the power of the Holy Spirit. The best true stories were in the two books that I have read about the work of the Holy Spirit in setting people free from heroin, crack cocaine and other addictions. The two books are *The Cross and the Switchblade* (by David Wilkerson) and *Chasing the Dragon* (by Jackie Pullinger). The work of these two people is amazing and they showed outstanding courage by working in dangerous conditions of drug use, crime and poverty.

St Paul says in 2 Timothy 1:6, "to fan into flame the gift of the Holy Spirit which is a Spirit of power (courage), love and self-control."

Punch line: Holy Spirit, Heaven's Waterfall!

**Let us pray**: Lord Jesus, our prayer on this Pentecost Sunday is that you give us a thirst and a craving for the Holy Spirit. Come, Holy Spirit, and enkindle in us the fire of your love. Come, Holy Spirit, we need you; set us free from our addictions and bad habits, so that we can enjoy our lives here on earth. We pray that the Holy Spirit be poured into our lives, on our children and our entire families. Amen.

CCC 799 Whether extraordinary or simple and humble, charisms are graces of the Holy Spirit which directly or indirectly benefit the Church, ordered as they are to her building up, to the good of men, and to the needs of the world.

# The Resurrection and the Life

Easter is the most important feast for Catholics, because we celebrate the only unprecedented event (never before or after has such a thing happened) in history—the Resurrection of Jesus from the dead! Halleluiah! Praise the Lord! We are called to be a 'Halleluiah' people, meaning to be filled with joy and happiness because of the victory of Christ over sin and death!

The Bible says that by dying on the cross and shedding blood for us, Jesus Christ defeated sin and death and conquered the world! That is why in John 3:16 we read, "God so loved the world that he sent his only begotten Son that whosoever believes in him will not perish but have eternal life." This is the promise and meaning of salvation, which is special for only those who believe that Jesus is the Son of God, according to the Bible.

There are four Gospel writers in the Bible: Matthew, Mark, Luke and John who testify or witness to the life, death and Resurrection of Jesus in detail. Normally, in a court of law, only two witnesses are required for evidence before a Judge. But here we have four witnesses, twice which is normally needed for good evidence!

The evidence for the Resurrection of Jesus is not written only in the Bible, but it was written outside the Bible by the first-century historian Flavius Josephus, in the history books of Israel. Other first century historians who wrote about Jesus are Gaius Suetonius and Publius Tacitus.

Remember five points beginning with the letter 'E' that give evidence or show that Jesus surely has risen from the dead.

1)  *The Execution: The evidence for the crucifixion and death of Jesus is airtight. Crucifixion was a very excruciating torture with huge blood loss. Nobody is known to have survived a Roman crucifixion. The JAMA in 1986 (published in Journal of American Medical Association – a renowned medical journal) examined the death of Jesus in detail and concluded without a doubt that Jesus was clearly dead before he was taken down from the cross. The piercing with a spear and blood and water ensuing from his side was postmortem evidence of the death of Jesus. Some people, especially from other religions, deny the death of Jesus, but the evidence for death is fool proof.*

2)  *The Empty Tomb: Everyone in the ancient world at that time 'agreed without any disagreement that the tomb was empty on the third day' (including Pharisees and the Romans). But they alleged that the 'disciples stole the body'. This argument has no basis because the disciples did not have the means or the motive or the opportunity to steal the body. Moreover, all the apostles were later martyred and they surely would not die for a cause that they knew not to be true.*

3) *Eyewitness accounts: The New Testament records that five hundred and fifteen people witnessed the risen Jesus and he appeared to five hundred people at the same time! As a result, the lives even of sceptics were transformed. When he appeared to others as in the reading today and last week, they touched him, ate with him and communicated with him. These were not events of wishful thinking or hallucinations. It was reality just as you see me and we see each other.*

4) *Early Records: The story of Jesus' resurrection was not a legend or a tale. It was a well-documented historical fact that is preserved for us in the New Testament documents and other non-Christian documents. The first written account of resurrection can go back very close to the event. Only about 24-36 months; these are reliable and authentic records. This was a news flash of more than historic proportion. We have more than 25,000 New Testament manuscripts and this is far more than any other historical book; with works of Homer being a very distant second. According to 'Textual Science', the Bible ranks as an invincible front runner for the authenticity of ancient texts including Scripture!*

5) *Emergence of the Christian Church: It is difficult to explain how the Christian Church exploded to life only a few weeks after the degrading death of Jesus in the very same place where he was crucified. How do you explain this apart from the Resurrection of Jesus? Peter spoke boldly, and nobody questioned his authority and three thousand people were added to the church that day.*

The historical analysis of the death and resurrection of Jesus is very strong. The truth is on our side and we Christians actually have an unfair advantage in the marketplace of spiritual ideas.

On Easter Sunday, the Catholic Church proclaims aloud to the world that Jesus is alive!

Punch line: Jesus is Alive!

**Let us pray**: Lord, we pray that the profound experience of your Resurrection to your disciples, may stir our hearts to believe that you are alive and seated at the right hand of the Father interceding for us poor sinners. We pray that at the name of Jesus every knee should bow and every tongue should confess that Jesus is Lord to the glory of the Father (Philippians 2:10-11). Amen.

CCC 1169 Therefore Easter is not simply one feast among others, but the "Feast of feasts," the "Solemnity of solemnities," just as the Eucharist is the "Sacrament of sacraments" (the Great Sacrament). St. Athanasius calls Easter "the Great Sunday" and the Eastern Churches call Holy Week "the Great Week." The mystery of the Resurrection, in which Christ crushed death, permeates with its powerful energy our old time, until all is subjected to him.

# The Humility of God

Today's reflection is about being a faithful servant of Jesus Christ. I would like to give a short sermon on what it means to be a servant and call for all disciples of Jesus to have a servant heart. The hallmark of a servant of God is to grow in the virtue of humility which is the opposite of pride.

There are six things the Lord hates (Proverbs 6:16). Firstly, the Lord hates haughty eyes, meaning a proud look. Just to remind you, that 'PRIDE' is the deadliest of sins, and it is the sin of Satan. In Isaiah 14, the accepted interpretation is that Satan says "I, I, I, I, I," five times, and then he is thrown out of heaven. There is no place for pride in the Kingdom of Heaven.

*Self is elevated in our culture today—self-satisfaction and self-reliance; I and my rights. Apparently, every day, over 90 million selfies are taken, and more than 24 billion selfies were uploaded on the internet, in a study done four years ago! For teenagers, this may be too low! St Paul teaches us to humble ourselves, to realise the gift and graciousness of God in our lives and helping others, even at the expense of our rights.*

An anecdote from the life of the well-known scientist Isaac Newton is presented here:

*Isaac Newton developed a beautiful concept of Mathematics and it was the mathematical study of a continuous change.*

*He wanted to give it a name, but unfortunately, nothing was clicking in his mind. He pondered, wondering, thinking over and over again but couldn't find a name. He woke up one early morning and went for a walk along the sea shore and a small pebble pricked his bare foot. He took out the pebble looked at it and then looked at the ocean and he had a great realisation or maybe a revelation.*

*He said, "the knowledge I have is small like this pebble and knowledge that exists in this world still open to discovery is like the ocean," which is incomparable to whatever little knowledge he had—this is the humility of Newton. Finally, Newton named his new theory as 'Calculus', which means a small pebble in Latin. Newton exemplified a beautiful statement in Sanskrit—'vidhyam dadati vinayam', which means, 'a person who is in real knowledge does not think that he knows everything but always humble so that he can learn more and more.' Friends, let us not become PROUD of whatever insignificant skills and expertise we've got, rather, let us be humble and open to learning more and more.*

The current body of scientific knowledge is only the size of a pebble when compared with the wisdom and power and glory of God. Unfortunately, this is not acknowledged by the secular world we live in. My son-in-law Sam, who is a specialist in hand plastic surgery, was sharing with me over breakfast, about an online journal article on hand surgery about the biomechanical function of the hand. The article ended with the concluding line that 'the intricate function of this amazing part of our body, the hand, could not have happened by chance but rather was created by an intelligent designer'. Unfortunately, the article was rejected because of inappropriate, unscientific language and its reference to a creator God.

The point I want to emphasise from my long experience of working as a psychiatrist for 30 years is that 'your faith in God should be far greater than your faith in achievements of science like the ocean and the pebble'. Incidentally, I retired from the NHS as a psychiatrist four years ago, and I hope to spend the rest of my life talking and sharing about the healing love of God, which is not only permanent but takes us into eternity.

This great God of ours humbled himself, when he became man in Christ Jesus – the Lamb of God. He is calling out to you today loud and clear to come into a personal loving relationship with him.

I've heard it said that rivers of grace from the Lord do not travel upstream to a proud man's heart, but rather the love of God, can be poured only downstream into a heart that has humbled itself. A humble person regards others as better than himself. This is from the letter of St Paul to Philippians 2:4, and it goes on to say 'look not to your own interests but to the interests of others'.

The following traits seen in a person, reveal the work of pride in our lives:

1)   *You take everything personally and prone to be easily offended.*
2)   *Your feelings are the most reasonable, making you overestimate your own capacity. You do not have an accurate view or understanding of yourself (rooted in pride) leading to fights and arguments (proverbs 3:13).*

3)  *Your desires are the most important. What you want, is what everybody else should want, leading to division (diabolic in nature).*

4)  *You always think the other person needs to apologise or change, whilst ignoring 'the plank in your own eye' (Matthew 7:3-5).*

5)  *You tend to be negative and critical, instead of being positive and grateful. Your negativity has resulted in alienating people in your life; people avoid you. The language of arrogance, is complaining and criticising, whilst the language of humility is gratitude and encouragement.*

6)  *You keep thinking of other people who need to hear this – "I'm so glad my spouse came with me today" because he's so critical and negative. You see the problem in others but not yourself; the pride of your heart has deceived you (Jeremiah 2:13).*

*A Common denominator for pride can be wealth – those who are rich prone to become arrogant. 1 Tim 6:17 reads: "As for those in the present age are rich, command them not to be haughty, or to set their hopes on the uncertainty of riches, but rather on God who richly provides us with everything for our enjoyment." 'Money' is so uncertain and can be a false god; insignificant in the scheme of eternity. People in Western countries, especially USA and UK, find a sense of security in finances rather than God. Remember that 85% of the world population live in substandard housing—no running water or electricity. For your information, money too is from God!*

*1 Corinthians 4:7 (paraphrased): "what are you so puffed up about? What do you have that God hasn't given you? And if all you have is from God, why act as though you have accomplished something on your own?"*

*This is the lens through which we should look at money. Keep in mind the following points and it will help us develop an attitude of humility:*

1) *We have made money on borrowed body and mind and borrowed air that we breathe.*

2) *You did not decide when you were born; it was God who chose you to live in this time in history!*

3) *Don't underestimate what God has allowed to happen in your life.*

4) *Don't miss the gracious gifts of God in your life and don't overestimate your effort in the success you have achieved.*

5) *Look for an opportunity every day to 'put someone else ahead of yourself'.*

6) *Give sacrificially and anonymously.*

7) *Repent of your pride and selfishness.*

There are three things you need to do!

1) Humble yourself!
2) Humble yourself!
3) Humble yourself!

Punch line: Humility pierces the heavens!

**Let us pray**: Lord, give us the grace to turn from denial to acceptance, from selfishness to selflessness and from pride to humility. Amen.

---

CCC 2559 "Prayer is the raising of one's mind and heart to God or the requesting of good things from God." But when we pray, do we speak from the height of our pride and will, or "out of the depths" of a humble and contrite heart? He who humbles himself will be exalted; humility is the foundation of prayer. Only when we humbly acknowledge that "we do not know how to pray as we ought," are we ready to receive freely the gift of prayer. "Man is a beggar before God."

# Jesus' Walk to Emmaus

This Sunday's Gospel is of particular interest to Catholics because in this true story of 'the two disciples walk to Emmaus' (Luke 24:13-35), the great importance of the Holy Mass is captured in amazing style, by the Lord Himself.

Actually, under the guidance of the Holy Spirit, when we read this story, it contains a perfect outline of the Holy Mass, that is so special and celebrated with reverence and awe by the Catholic Church.

'The Holy Mass' can be divided into two parts:

1) Part One is called 'The Liturgy of the Word' and has three subsections.
   a) The 'Entrance' of the priest into a gathering of people
   b) The 'Penance'—asking forgiveness for sins (Lord have mercy…) and Prayer of the Faithful (petitions)
   c) The 'Scripture (Bible) Readings' followed by a sermon (preaching) and Profession of faith (I believe…)

2) Part Two is called 'Liturgy of the Eucharist' and has three subsections.
   a) The 'Offertory'—bread, wine and other gifts offered to God

b) The 'Communion'—distribution of the body and blood of Christ

c) The 'Dismissal'—to go out and share the Good News with others

In the story of the Walk to Emmaus, we can see how this format of the Holy Mass was presented by Jesus in a hidden way which can be explained as follows:

## Part One

1) There is a gathering of people when two disciples are together (Matthew 18:20: "where 2 or 3 are gathered I'm in your midst"). Jesus who is the Eternal High Priest enters the scene (The Entrance) and joins the two disciples.

2) The disciples are downcast and show they are disappointed; burdened by their sins and their difficulties in life. They share with Jesus their disappointment and Jesus is there to accept their sorrow (Penance) and they explain all their problems to him (actually making a Petition Prayer).

3) Then Jesus opened their minds to hear the Scriptures; explaining to them all that was spoken about Him, starting from Moses to what all the prophets wrote about him in the Old Testament. They actually heard from the Bible, followed by a very long sermon from the lips of Jesus. When they heard the Word of God and the Sermon, it made their hearts burn within them.

**Part Two**

The disciples were so happy being with Jesus that they wanted him to stay with them longer. They were good hosts and they prepared a table for him, to share a meal with Jesus.

1) Jesus was now the chief guest and he was acting like a priest and presiding over the meal at the table. The table was in fact an altar on which the bread and wine were offered. The offertory was completed as they offered the bread and wine to Jesus.

2) Jesus blessed the bread and broke it (Jesus was actually saying the prayer of consecration, like a priest over the bread and wine) and gave it to his disciples. This is when they received the Holy Communion from the hands of Jesus Himself—there has never been a Mass like this one that Jesus Himself celebrated on earth, after his resurrection and before he ascended to Heaven. Such a blessed day for those two disciples!

3) As soon as they had had the communion, Jesus vanished from their sight because he was now present in the form of bread in the Holy Communion in their hearts. This was an amazing out-of-the-world experience, when they met Jesus, face to face and had communion with him—an unforgettable experience for them. They then go and tell the others about this blessed walk, they had with Jesus on the Road to Emmaus. This was how the first Holy Mass ended!

So, my dear friends, each time you participate in Mass remember and believe that Jesus comes and joins and walks with you. As you listen to the Bible reading, your hearts should burn with love and this experience becomes complete when at communion, he enters your heart and makes his home with you. So never miss the opportunity for Holy Mass— Heaven comes down to you!

Punch line: Eucharist – the Passover to Heaven!

**Let us pray**: Lord, help us to keep the Sabbath holy and to participate without fail in the celebration of the Lord's Supper in the Holy Mass, which is the source and summit of our Christian faith (Catechism of the Catholic Church 1324). Amen.

CCC 1331 Holy Communion, because by this sacrament we unite ourselves to Christ, who makes us sharers in his Body and Blood to form a single body. We also call it: the holy things (ta hagia; sancta) – the first meaning of the phrase "communion of saints" in the Apostles' Creed – the bread of angels, bread from heaven, medicine of immortality, viaticum…

# The Wisdom and Treasure of God

The key verses in this Sunday readings are:

1) How to discern between good and evil.
2) By turning everything to our good, God co-operates with those who love him.
3) The Kingdom of God is like a treasure hidden in a field.

The Lord is speaking to us, using the same words that he spoke to King Solomon about three thousand years ago: "Ask what you would like me to give you." King Solomon, unlike most people, did not ask for riches or long life or any other personal needs. He realised the most difficult task for a human being living in a fallen and sinful world is to have the understanding of how to discern or know the difference between good and evil. He asked God for wisdom (a discerning heart) so that he can differentiate between good and evil. King Solomon is known for his great wisdom which he received as a gift from God.

The Devil is described in the Bible as a cunning serpent, who deceived Adam and Eve to disobey God (Genesis 3:1) and as a roaring lion (2 Peter 5:7), looking for whom to devour. God told Cain that 'evil is crouching at your doorstep and you must overcome it' (Genesis 4:7). King Solomon realised that it is evil entering his life that can bring about his downfall. Therefore, his strength, success and might as a King will depend upon how successful he is in overcoming evil in his life. God endowed King Solomon with wisdom and he was immensely blessed by the Lord. It is Solomon who built the first Temple of Jerusalem for the Lord and it is described in the Bible as a spectacular piece of art.

Solomon was known most for his wisdom, but he was also blessed with riches. The Queen of Sheba hearing about the Wisdom of Solomon travelled a long way, to meet him and hear him speak. What she saw exceeded her expectation! Jesus quoted this story pointing to himself, Jesus said "something greater than Solomon is here" (Matthew 12:42)!

So, dear friends, first and foremost, ask God for wisdom and understanding to make the right choice in life (like saying no to drugs and alcohol and wrong relationships—all these cannot give you wisdom or riches!)

Secondly, be aware that our God is powerful and he can turn bad things that happen in our life into good, especially for those who are called according to his purpose (Romans 8:28). The only way we can show God that we love him is by keeping his commandments, because God's commandments are more precious than silver or gold. The love of God should take centre stage in our lives. We know from the life of King Solomon, that he did not ask for temporal worldly things, but worldly riches were also given to him when he asked God to give him wisdom.

Jesus says today that the Kingdom of God is like a treasure hidden in a field—it is worth more than all other worldly riches and attachments.

*I remember a movie I saw in my childhood called McKenna's Gold starring famous actors, Gregory Peck and Omar Sheriff. It is beautifully taken and action-packed movie, in which a motley crew of men and women set out in 'search of a canyon full of gold'—pursued by Apaches and the cavalry. A Sheriff is entrusted with a treasure map by a dying Indian, which he burns after committing it to memory. His secret holds out a promise of untold wealth, if he can trace the legendary lost canyon, but also makes him the target of ruthless fortune hunters.*

Basically, the sheriff who is the only one who knows where the gold is hidden, runs the risk of sacrificing his life to get the treasure. He was prepared to risk his life for the treasure. This is exactly what Jesus challenges us today. How much are we prepared to give up our worldly riches and comforts for the Kingdom of God? The Kingdom of God is that treasure, the McKenna's Gold, hidden in a canyon, and anything else you value in your life is worth giving up, in order to enter the Kingdom of God. The Kingdom of God is indeed "A Pearl of great price."

St Paul says in 2 Corinthians 4:7, "But we have this treasure in clay jars, so that it may be made clear that this extraordinary power belongs to God and does not come from us." The Kingdom of God, is having Christ, the wisdom and treasure of God, in our broken hearts (mere earthen vessels-the clay jars).

So, we learn today that wisdom from God is a very important gift. We must ask for it in prayer. Secondly, have the faith to believe that God exists and because we believe he exists, he can do the impossible and even turn bad into good. Thirdly, the Kingdom of God is the real treasure—we should not spare any effort and leave no stone unturned to make this treasure ours. When we have found it, make sure nobody robs it from us, by ensuring that it remains secure and safe in our hearts.

Punch Line: Life – a treasure hunt for Jesus!

**Let us pray**: We thank you Father for sending us your only begotten Son, Jesus Christ through whom you have revealed yourself to us. Come Holy Spirit, guide us in making right choices and decisions in our life, so that all that we need is added on to us (Matthew 6:33). We ask you Lord to shine your divine light for direction in our lives. Amen

CCC 474 By its union to the divine wisdom in the person of the Word incarnate, Christ enjoyed in his human knowledge the fullness of understanding of the eternal plans he had come to reveal. What he admitted to not knowing in this area, he elsewhere declared himself not sent to reveal.

# The Great Commission

The Scripture verses to consider in this reflection are:

Acts 3:15: "… and you killed the Author of life, whom God raised from the dead. To this we are witnesses."

Acts 3:19: "Repent therefore, and turn to God so that your sins may be wiped out…"

Luke 24:47: "… and that repentance and forgiveness of sins is to be proclaimed in his name to all nations." Luke 24:48: "You are witnesses of these things."

Today's readings are about the events that took place after the Resurrection of Jesus from the dead. Jesus appeared to the disciples and Peter is witnessing having seen the risen Jesus. Jesus himself demands the repentance and forgiveness of sins to be preached to all nations and that his followers should be witnesses to the Risen Christ and power in the name of Jesus.

'Jesus is alive' is the watchword especially during the Eastertide leading up to the Pentecost.

The two important points to take home:

1) Repent and believe
2) Witness that Jesus is alive

In my opinion, Christian life without witness becomes merely a religion to follow. But Christian faith in Jesus Christ combined with witness makes the faith come alive. The Catholic teaching is that, we need both faith and action, through which we are able to point to Christ. In James 2:24, we read: "we are not saved by faith alone"!

I now work as a Prison Chaplain and I have the opportunity to put my faith into action. My main intention is to be a witness or a signpost to Christ. It is only through the power of the Holy Spirit that we get power to witness.

A witness is a person who sees an event happening or had a special knowledge or experience of the event and his testimony of the event becomes evidence or proof for the event to have truly taken place. Christianity spread because people had a personal encounter with Jesus, leading to a bold witness of their belief and faith.

In my prison ministry, as a positive consequence of sharing the Gospel, an agnostic prisoner embraced the Catholic faith and he was baptised in the prison chapel. He was seeking God because he was convinced that it was God who saved him from death when he attempted suicide. As I shared the Gospel across closed doors, he wanted to know more. Eventually he requested me to teach him the Catholic faith, which I did for over five months and culminated in him receiving the Sacraments of Baptism, Confirmation and Holy Eucharist. This fruit of my ministry, gave me greater impetus to continue in prison ministry. In prison, there is great spiritual hunger.

I think it is impossible to become a witness if you remain in your sin. Jesus said at least twice 'sin no more; he said to stop sinning or less something worse might happen to you'. St John is again saying stop sinning and repent. My heart is full of thanksgiving to my God who in Jesus on the cross, reconciled me to himself.

After 60 years of life, I have no complaints but only thanksgiving to God.

Secondly, I have reaped the benefits of being obedient to God and to my parents—bread and butter Christianity. 'Love and obedience are like two sides of the same coin'. Acknowledge God and worship him alone—God and not science or the COVID vaccine. God's protection is very powerful and can work even through the vaccine. The vaccine and the virus keep changing. The only one who is changeless and ageless is our God revealed in Christ. Never substitute science for God, who is the source of science!

Another prisoner who was a lapsed Catholic, interacted with me. I shared with him the Catholic Christian faith, leading him to make a daily commitment to read the Bible. He started having a surge or increase in his faith. He started avidly reading the Bible, praying three rosaries daily, along with the Divine Mercy Chaplet and all prayers in a prayer book. He spent at least 3 hours in prayer every day and then also started fasting. He became filled with the Holy Spirit and he had a word of knowledge from the Holy Spirit. He was given the gift to compose Christian songs. He has written three songs. The first one is a classic, pure, undiluted, core Christian message in the lyrics of a song called 'Turn to God'.

If the Holy Spirit can work in a prison, he can most certainly work in all of us.

Be compassionate and go the extra mile, in your place of work or study, to help a person, especially if there is a genuine need. This is because for most people, you will be the only Gospel that they will read. They should be able to see that extra special spark in you that sets you apart from others— you should love the way Jesus taught us to love. Not just sticking to the job description, but crossing the border and reaching out— a love beyond borders. This is a simple way in which all Christians can be a witness to Jesus. Do this not only in your workplace, school or college but in our homes too. Also, show genuine love among our own families and be abounding in marital love.

Witnessing to the love of God can bring us the peace that Jesus promised. He said, "In me you will have peace, but in this world, you will have trouble, but do not be afraid because I have conquered the world" (John 16:33).

Finally have a committed time for prayer and trust in the Lord—have a prayerful and trusting heart. 'Those who trust in the Lord are like Mount Zion, they shall never be shaken' (psalm 125:1). Like the prisoner who received gifts from the Holy Spirit, as he spent long hours in prayer, you too should have a commitment to prayer and reading the Bible and this is the testimony of so many saints.

In this Dark Age, there is no room to be of lukewarm faith, but we must strive to step up another gear. Otherwise, the wickedness and deception of this world, is likely to overwhelm our lives, taking away its meaning and purpose.

Punch line: Be a sign post for Jesus!

**Let us pray**: Lord, we pray that you empower us with your Holy Spirit, to be witnesses to your grace and power working in our lives. May the Christian testimony echoing through the centuries, continue to spread to those yet to hear the message of Salvation. We make this prayer through Christ our Lord. Amen.

---

CCC 849 The missionary mandate. "Having been divinely sent to the nations that she might be 'the universal sacrament of salvation,' the Church, in obedience to the command of her founder and because it is demanded by her own essential universality, strives to preach the Gospel to all men": "Go therefore and make disciples of all nations, baptizing them in the name of the Father and of the Son and of the Holy Spirit, teaching them to observe all that I have commanded you; and Lo, I am with you always, until the close of the age."

# Pray Continually

Jesus exhorts us to pray continually and he gives us permission to persist in our prayers and never give up—Jesus allows us to pester him!

For me, prayer became a joy and a delight, after I was baptized in the Holy Spirit in 1993. In Romans 8:26, St Paul says that the 'Spirit helps us to pray because we don't know how to pray'. I love the Charismatic Renewal in the Catholic Church because it gives me the freedom in my spirit to worship him in spirit and in truth (John 4:24).

1) What is Christian prayer?
2) Does God always answer prayer?
3) Practical hint to keep prayer life alive

So, what is Christian prayer? Turn to Ephesians 2:18 and it reads "we have access to the Father through Jesus Christ by the Spirit—the Father, the Son and the Holy Spirit."

It is only through belief in the true identity of Jesus Christ and having faith in his name that prayer becomes meaningful and achieves its purpose. Prayer with faith in Christ leads to establishing a personal relationship with God.

Prayer basically is communication with God. Communication is so basic in any relationship and without good communication, we encounter all sorts of problems. A common problem of poor communication and disharmony in relationship is divorce. Therefore, my dear friends, the most important activity for Christians is prayer. It is the only thing that can keep your spirit alive; it is the breath for your soul. Belief without prayer is like having a body without breath. A person who has no prayer life is in actual fact spiritually dead. Prayer is of utmost importance.

*So, does God always answer prayer? I believe the answer is yes, but we don't always get what we want. For a start, God can't act in a way that's inconsistent with his nature. In other words, you can't pray that 2 + 2 will equal anything other than 4 because it can't—that's a mathematical system that is set up, and that's how it works.*

*We all have sympathy, I think, with the small boy's desperate and doomed prayer emerging from the geography exam, praying: "Oh dear God, please make Paris the capital of Turkey! It can't work!"*

*I think sometimes in terms of relationships, as well, he shuts doors. I heard about Billy Graham's wife, Ruth Graham, who was been happily married to Billy Graham for over 50 years— she told an audience in Minneapolis: "God has not always answered my prayers. If he had, I would have married the wrong man, several times!"*

*Another common reason for unanswered prayer is because of sin. When we cherish sin in our heart or harbour grudges and resentment and remain hard-hearted and unforgiving, the Lord says he cannot answer. Isaiah 59:1-2 says 'it is not because my hand is too short to help you or because I am deaf and cannot hear, but rather your sins have separated me from you'.* If this block happens, the best medicine is to go to confession as soon as possible!

A personal favourite Scripture for me is Jeremiah 33:3. This is my free phone number to the Lord because it says 'Call on me and I will answer you'. The Lord does not say I might answer you or I may answer you. He gives us a promise "I will answer you." We can have faith in the promises in the Bible, we can have faith because of the work of Jesus and we can have faith because of our experience of the Holy Spirit in our lives.

If we have the faith that Jesus expects us to have, then we should be people who persevere and persist in prayer.

Here's a true story to illustrate this point:

*I once again recount the story of a mother called Monica who was a Christian woman and she was having real problems with her rebellious teenage son. He was lazy; he was bad-tempered, a cheat, a liar, a thief. And, later on, though outwardly he became very respectable as a lawyer, his life was dominated by worldly ambition and a desire to make money. His morals were loose; he lived with several different women and had a son by one of them. And, at one stage, he joined some weird religious sort of cult and adopted all kinds of strange practices.*

*And, throughout this time, this mother just continued to pray for him and her prayer was 'let your kingdom come into his life'. And one day, the Lord gave her a vision and she just wept as she prayed because she saw the light of Jesus Christ on him and his face was just smiling at her with great joy. And that encouraged her to keep on praying. But it was nine years after this vision, that her son finally gave his life to Christ, at the age of 28.*

*That man's name was Augustine, 'Saint Augustine', converted in 386 AD, ordained in 391 AD, served as bishop in 396 AD, perhaps the greatest theologian of the church! And St Augustine always attributed his conversion to the prayers of his mother. His mother's prayers literally changed the course of history!*

In conclusion, prayer life is akin to using a mobile phone. Make sure you know which number to dial (333) and have the Jesus app downloaded on your phone and the wireless internet server is the Holy Spirit, so you will be sure that you are connected to your Father in heaven (the world wide web!).

Also, make sure to keep your prayer life mobile phone charged, throughout the day and night, by praying continually. Do not switch it off, but you can leave it on silent if you're in a meeting. And, if your prayer life phone is not working, do not call Talk-Talk Telecom for help, instead go to confession immediately and ask the Lord for forgiveness, to quickly re-establish the connection.

There are three things you need to do to keep the Holy Spirit alive in your heart:

1) Pray
2) Pray
3) Pray

Punch line: Prayer – the Stairway to Heaven!

**Let us pray**: Lord our God, we pray that you bless us with a spirit of prayer so that our channel of communication with you will always remain open. Help us to abide in faith, in virtue and in the teaching of the Church and Scripture. Let us never lose heart in our fervour for prayer as this is the only thing you have asked us to do continually. We make this prayer through Christ our Lord. Amen.

---

CCC 2744 Prayer is a vital necessity. Proof from the contrary is no less convincing: if we do not allow the Spirit to lead us, we fall back into the slavery of sin. How can the Holy Spirit be our life if our heart is far from him?

Nothing is equal to prayer; for what is impossible it makes possible, what is difficult, easy... For it is impossible, utterly impossible, for the man who prays eagerly and invokes God ceaselessly ever to sin.

Those who pray are certainly saved; those who do not pray are certainly damned.

---

# Epilogue

Ironically, as I pen the last few lines, I am recovering from the throes of a third episode of Covid-19! The Corona virus is invisible to the naked eye but its presence is known by the effect it produces in the human organism with the characteristic clinical syndrome of fever, cough, loss of senses of taste and smell along with or without other features such as lethargy, diarrhoea and a number of other clinical manifestations! Similarly, we know that the invisible God we serve is present through the manifestations of the Holy Spirit, working in our lives, producing the good fruits contributing to a wholesome and abundant lifestyle. On the contrary, we know the dark side of life with anger, dissension, quarrels, immorality, drunkenness and the like, pointing to the presence of the evil one, doing damage behind the scenes. Unfortunately, unlike the corona virus that can be found by testing in a laboratory, our God who created us cannot be measured in a test tube! St Augustine wisely said 'it is better to believe and then understand, rather than to understand and then believe'. St John the Evangelist says he wrote the Gospel, so that we may believe that Jesus, the Son of God, is the Messiah and through believing, you may have life in his name (John 20:30).

# Internet References of Real-Life Stories

1) Corrie Ten Boom: story of forgiveness,
   https://guideposts.org/positive-living/guideposts-classics-corrie-ten-boom-forgiveness/
2) Fr Kolbe and Franciszek Gajowniczek in Auschwitz,
   https://www.nytimes.com/1995/03/15/obituaries/franciszek-gajowniczek-dead-priest-died-for-him-at-auschwitz.html
3) Nicky Cruz,
   https://en.wikipedia.org/wiki/Nicky_Cruz
4) Jesuit priests who survived Hiroshima atomic bomb,
   https://www.ncregister.com/blog/the-jesuit-priests-who-survived-hiroshima
5) Real-life story of Shane Taylor,
   https://www.youtube.com/watch?v=GlLD6ddWPXg
6) https://youtu.be/Pd_SuVcEOGA?si=sWbGXGO4
   Powerful Reasons for Jesus' resurrection – 5 E's Evidence YouTube video TruthIsLife7
   **Stories of Abraham Lincoln, Ruth Graham, Answered Prayer, St Monica, Shane Taylor and Pippa wife of Nicky Gumbel** from the Alpha Course and related publicationswww.htb.org.uk based in Holy Trinity Brompton (Church of England), London
7) Communion on the Moon

https://youtu.be/reErZrm03eE?si=IDgI6_6gMIY18d
tm

8) Lanciano Miracle –
https://www.catholiceducation.org/en/culture/catholic-contributions/the-miracle-of-lanciano.html

9) https://youtu.be/57ZnDKN2S1U story of Isaac Newton and his humility by Anantha Vallabha Das

10) https://youtu.be/vOGJ6irhBiE?si=Xu7CDr0v6Hlb Fulton Sheen-three kinds of love

11) https://g.co/kgs/TRXv4J Mackenna's Gold Film Synopsis

12) ahttps://youtu.be/7RVpBtCbzr4 Humility over arrogance-Kyle Idleman

**Reference Books**

*New Revised Standard Version: Holy Bible*
*Catechism of the Catholic Church*
*The Lamb's Supper:* Scott Hahn
*Hail Holy Queen:* Scott Hahn
*The Questions of Life:* Nicky Gumbel
*Mere Christianity:* C.S. Lewis
*The Cross and the Switchblade:* David Wilkerson
*Words to Love by…:* Mother Teresa
*Run Baby Run:* Nicky Cruz
*Faith and Reason:* John Paul *II*
*Chasing the Dragon:* Jackie Pullinger